MV *Isle of Lewis*

MARK NICOLSON

Islands Book Trust

Published in 2016 by the Islands Book Trust

www.theislandsbooktrust.com

ISBN: 978-1-907443-69-5

Text © Mark Nicolson

Islands Book Trust
Laxay Hall
Laxay
Isle of Lewis
HS2 9PJ
Tel: 01851 830316

Typeset by Erica Schwarz (www.schwarz-editorial.co.uk)
Cover design by Raspberry Creative Type, Edinburgh
Printed and bound by Martins the Printers, Berwick upon Tweed

This book is dedicated to the memory of

Colin Stuart Paterson CBE

29 July 1932 – 14 April 2013

Former soldier and long running managing director
of Caledonian MacBrayne from 1983 to 1997,
and the man who brought the *Isle of Lewis* into the world

Contents

/cont.

Contents

Foreword

MARK NICOLSON, a native of the island of Lewis, attended Sgoil a' Bhac primary school. In May 2006, I gave a talk to the pupils on the history of Caledonian MacBrayne and Mark was present. He tells me the talk fired his enthusiasm for CalMac, and one of the results is this book. He is probably the greatest admirer of the vessel named after his home island – at the time, the largest and fastest in the CalMac fleet. Mark's strength, however, is not only his enthusiasm, but a genuine sense of history and an ability to communicate this to his readers. His research has been fastidious in every way and the scope of the book is vast. He not only chronicles the events in the life of the *Isle of Lewis*, he also gives a plethora of background information; for example he delves into the previous history of the services to Stornoway, the technical details of the ship, a detailed description of her features and even the story of her various Masters.

A Bachelor of Science of the University of the Highlands & Islands, Mark has a fine style of writing. He has the capacity to convey meticulous detail in an interesting way, and has produced a collection of illustrations seldom if ever surpassed. Not only that, he has painstakingly followed up all copyright issues, no matter how difficult or obscure.

This book will certainly be a very worthwhile addition to the extensive library of literature for those enthusiastic about maritime history. Hopefully, it will be the first of many from his pen, and we look forward eagerly to Mark's future publications.

Ian McCrorie

Acknowledgements

IN WRITING THIS BOOK, I am indebted to the many people gracious enough to assist with its production. First of all, I thank Ian McCrorie, Donald Meek and John MacLeod for carefully reading the text, making corrections where necessary, and for offering useful advice. For my main research, I have made use of the comprehensively detailed Annual Reviews by the Clyde River Steamer Club, as well as the twice yearly newsletter produced by the West Highland Steamer Club – the painstaking effort of the late Jim Aikman Smith, and latterly Derek Crawford. Extra assistance and thanks are given to Iain Don Maciver, Bob Morrison, Colin Tucker, Colin J. Smith, Jack Kernahan, Lawrence Macduff, Alex Morrison and Michael MacLennan, with small amounts of information having also been provided from my own personal knowledge. I again thank Ian McCrorie, for agreeing to compose the Foreword.

The photographs used have either come from my own collection, or have been supplied for reproduction by others – most particularly Michael MacLennan and Jack Kernahan – and I have acknowledged all of the sources with their inclusion at the end of each caption. Photographs taken by the late Jim Aikman Smith have been bequeathed to the National Records of Scotland, and I thank them for allowing permission of their use, using the reference GD469. I also thank Andrew Clark of the Clyde River Steamer Club for giving permission to reproduce the photographs of Colin Paterson and the original *Loch Seaforth*.

I feel extremely privileged to have produced this account of one of my favourite ships of all time. The *Isle of Lewis* would remain the largest and fastest motor vessel ever built for CalMac and its predecessors until 2014. Although many others were built during her lifetime, none were able to exceed her specifications. I do have other favourite fleet members, but the *Isle of Lewis* stood out for me the most, as she was the ship which started my interest in CalMac, as well as being such a faithful servant to my home island, and I have not felt this kind of affection for any other ship in the world.

Mark Nicolson

ONE

Stornoway's Shipping History before 1995

From Monday 31 July 1995 until Saturday 29 August 2015, Caledonian MacBrayne's 'marine motorway' between Stornoway and Ullapool across the North Minch was operated by what was their largest and fastest ship ever built, the *Isle of Lewis*. She was the first 'purpose-built' vessel for Stornoway since the shorter route to Ullapool was established in March 1973. This replaced the longer mail run from Stornoway to Mallaig via Kyle of Lochalsh – operated most famously by the iconic David MacBrayne mailboat *Loch Seaforth*.

Regular, timetabled passenger services anywhere only began with the age of steam and Henry Bell's pioneering *Comet*, which launched the world's first – from Greenock to Glasgow – in 1812. Even the most powerful ferries today have on occasion to retreat before boisterous Scottish storms; in the days of sail the briefest passage was prone to delay, disruption and occasional tragedy. One early historian of Clyde steamers dryly records that, prior to the advent of boilers and paddle-wheels, from Glasgow the 'conveyance of goods and passengers to places more remote than Greenock was ... the Packet, which, with a fair wind, could reach the Isle of Bute in three days, but, when adverse, thought it "not wonderful" to plough the billowy main for as many weeks!' Shipwreck or sinking on passage to Lewis was frequent; one tragedy, in November 1824, saw the drowning of Rev. Simon Fraser, minister of Stornoway and one of the most important men on the island.

It was Sir James Matheson, though – having bought Lewis in 1844 – who in 1846 laid on the first steamship service, with the little paddler

Mary Jane built especially for passage between Stornoway and Poolewe. He sold her on in 1851, for he lost much money annually on the venture and received no subsidy from the Post Office. She never again sailed to Lewis. She was acquired by David Hutcheson Ltd in 1857 and in turn, in 1879, by the successor-company commanded by Hutcheson's partner, David MacBrayne, who subsequently enlarged her and renamed her as the *Glencoe* – withdrawn at last from passenger service only in 1931, still with her original engine and in her eighty-sixth year. She is still affectionately recalled on Skye for this forbidding notice in her cheapest, 'steerage' saloon, which read:

> *This Cabin has Accommodation for 90 Third-class Passengers,*
> *when not occupied by Sheep, Cattle or Other Encumbrances.*

Sir James tried again with a fitful mail-service by the paddler *Ondine*, this time from Stornoway to Ullapool, in later decades, but as a new Victorian tourism industry burgeoned Stornoway was most readily reached, from 1855, by taking Hutcheson's new paddle-steamer *Clansman* directly from Glasgow, by Oban and Skye and untold ports in between, at a leisurely thirteen knots. After her wreck in 1869, a second and very attractive *Clansman* – a single-engined screw ship – appeared in 1870 and would serve for nearly forty years on the same passage; leaving Glasgow every Monday and returning on Saturday morning. A still bonnier though very similar ship, the *Claymore* – the first vessel built for David MacBrayne's new management – joined her in 1881, leaving Glasgow each Thursday and returning on Wednesdays. In 1909 the *Clansman* was scrapped and, though the *Claymore* would sail on until her own demise in 1931, the bulk passenger-service from Glasgow was latterly summer-only – though, until as recently as November 1976 and the demise of the last MacBrayne cargo ship, the *Loch Carron*, a direct run from Glasgow to Stornoway survived.

A new railway from Inverness reached first to Stromeferry in 1870, then Kyle of Lochalsh in 1897 – and a line from Glasgow by Fort William finally reaching Mallaig in 1901 – far more convenient journeys were possible, and options for travel to Lewis were further expanded, though the continued popularity of the Glasgow route (at least for summer gentry) for many years denied these West Highland railheads a substantial or even adequate ship from Stornoway. The second-hand paddler *Great Western* inaugurated sailings to Stromeferry in 1891 – she was later enlarged, and renamed *Lovedale* – and, in 1904, she was replaced by the little single-screw vessel *Sheila*. Though slow, tiny and uncomfortable, she was of legendary reliability and, for over two decades, 'fought and defied the Minch, summer and winter, on the passage between Kyle of Lochalsh and Stornoway with passengers, cargo and mails, and the occasions when "weather and circumstances" were so utterly outrageous that she did not venture out were few and far between.

The wreck of the *Sheila*, north of Applecross, on New Year's Day 1927, was fortunately without loss of life, but was the first of a chain of disasters during that year – referred to as MacBrayne's 'annus horribilis', which culminated with the destruction of the *Grenadier* by fire at Oban in September where her master and two other crew members lost their lives – which finally broke the private MacBrayne concern financially. By 1929 it was reconstructed with much public money and a hefty stake of State ownership and only then had sufficient capital, for the first time in many years, to build large modern ships. After a two-year interregnum with such steamers as the *Clydesdale*, the *Chieftain* and the *Loch Garry* on the Stornoway passage, the first grand new craft was the twinscrew vessel *Lochness*, which took up service from Stornoway to Kyle and Mallaig in August 1929, 'a fine sea boat and as far as the comfort of her passengers and crew were concerned far excelled the *Sheila*'. By the late 1930s, however, she was a little too small, and the Second World War delayed her eventual replacement.

That was the *Loch Seaforth* of 1947, built by Denny's of Dumbarton, also twin-screw, and the first motor ship to serve Stornoway of fair speed, handsome accommodation and cargo-capacity and rather stately appearance. Unfortunately, like all British ships of her era, she was built with very poor scrap-steel and by the late 1960s and in the age of the car-ferry, became more and more obsolete as well as embarrassingly accident-prone. Indeed, from late 1964 she was annually relieved by a new hoist-loading car ferry, the *Clansman*, one of three sisters furnished for MacBrayne's by the Government; with a secret role besides as floating nuclear-shelters in the event of national emergency.

It was growing increasingly obvious both that island freight was shifting away from rail or cargo-boat transit to preferred short-sea crossings and maximal use of roads and that a growing tourist business preferred to take their the cars with them. The traditional mailboat, loading everything by crane and chugging from some distant mainland railhead, was less and less suitable. But early car ferry development was hampered by restricted public funds and the complexities of local pier ownership. Hoist-loading ferries – cars driving on by side-ramps to a platform that could be lowered up and down as the tide decreed – could use conventional piers, but at extreme low tides the process was cumbersome and the weight and length of vehicles conveyed most restricted.

The *Loch Seaforth* was finally displaced in May 1972 – she would sink, in farcical circumstances, at Tiree the following spring – by a still newer ship, the 1970 car-ferry *Iona*, designed originally for an involved service from Kintyre to Islay with runs besides to Jura, Gigha and Colonsay. She was the first drive-through roll-on roll-off ferry built for David MacBrayne Ltd, which, since 1969, had been wholly in state ownership and run in tandem by the new Scottish Transport Group (STG) with the Caledonian Steam Packet Co. Ltd (CSP) on the Clyde. She featured bow and stern ramps and a side-loading hoist. Unfortunately, there were some elementary design-faults; the bow-visor was not even watertight, there were no sleeping-berths and the passenger accommodation was very poor.

The STG were now committed to a new car ferry crossing across the Minch to Ullapool and construction of linkspans began, but such was the antipathy to the *Iona* that it was decided to replace her with a radically rebuilt *Clansman*, which duly arrived at the Ailsa yard at Troon in October 1972 for major surgery. Besides, the New Year of 1973 brought significant organisational change, the CSP being renamed Caledonian MacBrayne Ltd and assuming direct ownership (with a new livery) of most of the combined MacBrayne and CSP fleets, and only a few MacBrayne craft on uneconomic routes being excepted.

The *Iona* maintained a hoist-loading service from Stornoway to Kyle and Mallaig till 26 March 1973, when she inaugurated the new linkspan at Ullapool and the link to the old railheads finally ceased. It was May, though, before the Stornoway linkspan was ready, and the handover to the *Clansman* on 29 June proved fraught – the *Iona* had just broken down, the *Clansman* herself broke down and the *Columba*, the third and final of the 1964 trio, had only just arrived to address the emergency when she broke down too.

The *Clansman* duly recovered. Lengthened by thirty feet, she looked rather liner-ish, with pleasant passenger accommodation and sleeping-berths. She was able to carry some sixty cars or their equivalent, and was an initial success. It grew rapidly evident, though, that the blithe decision not to re-engine her had left the ship distinctly underpowered and – more surprisingly – that she was too small, as local hauliers took avidly to the new service.

The solution was unexpected. On 12 November 1973, the STG announced they had bought a large drive-through car ferry under construction at Bergen in Norway, still on the 'stocks' therefore early enough to be completed to the very strict British safety standards. Named the *Suilven* after a well-known peak in Sutherland, she was launched on 19 April 1974. The sleek new ferry could carry 120 cars and was certificated for 408 passengers on a Class IIA certificate. After calling at Gourock 'to show the flag' – she was the largest ferry to date in the fleet – she reached Stornoway on 29 August. Though scheduled to give an inaugural cruise for invited guests the following day, she had to immediately enter service in place of a broken-down *Clansman* instead.

After her introduction, and some early problems with her electronic engine controls, the *Suilven* became a popular and reliable asset to the Lewis islanders, who quickly warmed to her. She was a very sturdy sea boat, regularly venturing out into atrocious seas which saw the majority of her fleet mates safely tied up. She had two vulnerabilities; an unpleasant roll in heavy seas, which was reduced after her first overhaul at Greenock, when she was fitted with stabilisers and severely limited passenger accommodation. With anything near a full complement there were not nearly enough seats for all on board and, though quite acceptable in a Scandinavian context, the combined lounge and bar was undesirable in a West Highland one. Management should have anticipated this. CalMac's former managing director John Whittle later confessed, "that this would cause embarrassment to the temperate passengers, but the problem has been resolved by partitioning ... to create an alcohol-free area."

The *Suilven* attracted national fame when she featured in a 1987 Grampian Television documentary about Stornoway, in which one of her masters, John MacDonald, was interviewed on the bridge by television personality Art Sutter. Despite only serving Lewis for most of her CalMac career, the *Suilven* visited the Uig triangle a few times for different purposes. Firstly, she gave an emergency sailing from Lochmaddy to Uig in March 1988 after the *Hebridean Isles* broke down. This was followed by an overnight visit to Tarbert in August 1989 after Stornoway's linkspan broke down, and finally a second call to Lochmaddy in August 1995 whilst *en route* to her final overhaul in home waters at Troon. She also served the Oban-Craignure route for ten days in October 1989, as the *Isle of Mull*'s larger passenger capacity was required for the Mòd in Lewis that month. The *Suilven* was assisted at Oban by another 1974-built vessel, the cult favourite *Pioneer*.

Sadly, by the early 1990s, the *Suilven* was beginning to show her age, compared with newer ships introduced in recent years, and it was clear she was becoming increasingly inadequate for the crossing on which she was so much appreciated. Her accommodation was very outdated for the new decade; the luxury and comfort of the modern *Isle of Mull*, the relief ship at Stornoway from 1989 to 1998, showed great contrast to her increasingly dated Norwegian-built consort. The *Suilven*'s vehicle capacity had been reduced to eighty-five, following strict new deadweight regulations that prohibited the use of her mezzanine decks. In any event, so many tall commercial vehicles were now being borne that they could scarcely be used at all. Another worry was that her fourteen knot maximum speed now seemed too slow – still only allowing three and a half hours on passage. And off-season commercial traffic continued to grow remorselessly. In early winters, the *Suilven* only needed to make one return trip a day. From January 1979 a second crossing was added on Tuesdays and Thursdays but she came under ever-increasing pressure of traffic. The first hint of a replacement vessel came about as early as 1988, but it would be early 1993 before an official announcement was made by the company.

Two

Enter *Isle of Lewis*

A Replacement is Ordered

THE FIRST OFFICIAL ANNOUNCEMENT of a replacement for the *Suilven* was made in Stornoway on 18 May 1993, but this news came as little surprise to anyone. What the Lewis islanders now required was a large vessel that was capable of carrying as much of the anticipated high level of passengers and vehicles in a single crossing as possible. The new vessel was also expected to meet very high demands, especially when dealing with the large amount of heavy goods travelling to Lewis. She was to be twenty-two feet longer than the recently-launched vessel for Arran, the *Caledonian Isles*, with a length overall of just over 101 metres, thus making her the largest vessel in the fleet. The design would be similar to that of the *Caledonian Isles* – two main differences being that the new ship would be double-funnelled, and would not feature an external forward deck for passengers. Her width was increased, from the normal breadth of 15.8m, to just over 18.5m. This would consciously limit her ability to serve on other routes, as a great deal of existing piers around the network were not adapted to suit her. This was a notable departure from the long-established Company principle of designing broadly versatile ships that could readily be 'cascaded' to other routes when replaced by larger vessels. Her increased beam meant that in order to unload at Ullapool, the stern ramp had to be off-set to port, and to unload at Stornoway, the forward section of the bow ramp had to be off-set to starboard, although the ramp itself was fixed in the centre of the ship. It was obvious that the pier at Ullapool – already extended once for the *Suilven* – would have to be lengthened again; and the Stornoway Pier & Harbour Commission prepared to build a completely new ferry terminal.

She would also be the last ship in the fleet to date to feature a fully enclosed car deck, which would affect the carrying of hazardous cargo on sailings with high numbers of passengers on board. However, most of the hazardous goods for Lewis were carried from Uig to Tarbert on the *Hebridean Isles* as an alternative, before continuing on a 37 mile drive to Stornoway. This had always been the norm with the *Suilven*. Bottled gas, until the mid-1990s, could not be borne on passenger ferries at all. It was also hoped that the new ship would be able to introduce regular Sunday sailings, something that the islanders had always been campaigning for, in spite of the need to respect the Sabbath in Lewis and Harris. This was problematic. Only a tiny fraction – in the late 1980s, just one man – pressed publicly for such sailings, and it was the late 1990s before the real lobby for Sunday crossings developed on Lewis. On 13 July 1993, CalMac received the official go-ahead for the new vessel from Westminster, permitting the placing of the £16 million contract with the shipbuilder offering the keenest tender. Fourteen concerns sought the order, two of which were based in Scotland.

On 22 September 1993, it was announced that the contract had been awarded to Ferguson Shipbuilders of Port Glasgow, which thus secured their first CalMac order since building two new Kyleakin ferries in 1991; the *Loch Dunvegan* and *Loch Fyne*. At the time of winning the order, Ferguson's were in the process of building new ferries for Red Funnel; the *Red Falcon* and *Red Osprey*, both destined to operate between Southampton and the Isle of Wight. CalMac have had a very good relationship with Ferguson's over the years, and many of their vessels have been built by the yard – the most recent of which were the revolutionary battery-powered sisters *Hallaig* and *Lochinvar*. The last major unit for CalMac built by Ferguson's before 1995 had been the *Lord of the Isles*, and the shipyard orders had brought huge increases to the economically depressed town of Port Glasgow over the years. The late Colin Paterson, then managing director of CalMac, confirmed that he was "absolutely delighted" to place the order with Ferguson's, and was confident that the yard would construct an "excellent ship." Around sixty workers were given the task of constructing the new vessel, destined to be Ferguson's largest product to date. Work started almost immediately on what would be temporarily known as yard number 608, with the steel cutting commencing before the end of the year. On 23 February 1994, the keel was laid, while the Red Funnel ferries underwent fitting out. The new CalMac vessel had to include either 'Isle' or 'Isles' somewhere in her name, once again adhering to Colin Paterson's controversial policy for all new major units, which was criticised as being boring, and giving the impression vessels were operating wildly off-station. She would indeed be the last such ship to be named. As a result, her name was obvious. Despite various other suggestions from islanders, she was named directly after the island she was destined to serve, as reported in the *West Highland Free Press* on 1 July 1994.

With her name settled, the new ship continued to take shape on the stocks overlooking Newark Castle as 1995 dawned, although the painting of her hull and superstructure were yet to be finished. From outside the yard, her enormous size gave the impression that the bow visor was poking right over the top of the yard offices, and that she was lying right on the main road into Port Glasgow. In February, it was announced that the *Suilven* would be sold from CalMac service, rather than retained, as the ageing vessel would soon fall short of stringent new British safety standards and the cost of upgrading her would therefore be prohibitive. Terms for her sale were concluded in May, when a deal was made with Strait Shipping Limited of Wellington, New Zealand. She would be destined to leave in the late summer when her replacement took over at Stornoway.

The Royal Launch, Fitting Out and Sea Trials

On 18 April, despite the fact that the fitting out and further painting of her rear upper superstructure had yet to start, the new vessel was ready for launching, five weeks ahead of schedule, thus demonstrating the capability of the workers at Ferguson's. At 1455, before a crowd of almost a thousand, HRH Princess Alexandra spoke the words, "I name this ship *Isle of Lewis*. May God bless her and all who sail in her", before smashing the champagne against the hull and sending the new ship on her way. As she slid into the Clyde, the *Isle of Lewis* tilted wildly to port, the result of a collapsed bow support, but managed to remain upright, and was then manoeuvred by two tugs to the fitting out berth. Taking charge of a special cruise for invited guests and CalMac personnel from Gourock to see the launch was the *Juno*, the second of the three streakers, scrapped along with her sister *Jupiter* in 2011. The launch ceremony was covered by Scottish Television's 'Scotland Today' news programme later that evening.

Fitting out took place throughout May and June, and included a single week at Greenock's Garvel drydock from 12 to 19 June, although she spent most of the time at Ferguson's newly-built fitting-out berth. All internal areas were fully furnished, with completion of seating, décor and various pieces of electrical and bridge equipment. After 'undocking' from the Garvel on 19 June, the *Isle of Lewis* carried out preliminary trials off the Tail of the Bank, where, at 85% power, she managed to achieve a speed of 17.5 knots. Her full speed trials took place on the Skelmorlie mile the following month. On 11 July, she ran at 85% as before, but this time, she was able to achieve 18.47 knots, before berthing overnight at Greenock's Ocean Terminal. She undertook her last day of sea trials on 12 July, where, at 100% power, her two Mirrlees Blackstone K6 Majors finally gave her the top speed of 18.92 knots, which thus made her the fastest-ever motor vessel for Caledonian MacBrayne or any of its predecessors. The record had previously been held by the *Lord of the Isles*, which was capable of 16 knots. The *Isle of Lewis*'s top speed astern was as high as 12.4 knots, almost as fast as the *Suilven*'s top speed ahead! She thus made a triumphant return to Ferguson's at 2105, hugely impressing the shipyard personnel with her performance. Thirteen days of final fitting-out work followed.

Port Glasgow Departure and Ardrossan Sojourn

The *Isle of Lewis* was completed and ready for delivery for the last full week of July 1995, twenty-two months since the order was first placed. She was noted for being the first new CalMac ship to comply with major upgrades of the regulations for Safety of Lives At Sea (SOLAS) whereas existing vessels had to be modified to comply with the new laws, which had been upgraded following the horrendous loss of life experienced in recent shipping tragedies including the sinking of the *Estonia* in the Baltic Sea in September 1994, and the capsizing of the *Herald of Free Enterprise* off Zeebrugge in March 1987. The causes of these two tragedies were bow-related, and as a result, the *Isle of Lewis* received significant attention to her internal bow structure during her construction. As always, safety is the most important priority of any shipping company, and CalMac have always taken the safety of their crews and passengers very seriously indeed.

There was unexpected controversy over her name. Rumour spread – and reached the press – of a sixteenth century prophecy by Kenneth MacKenzie, a Lewis-born clairvoyant remembered as the Brahan Seer. He had supposedly forecast that the 'Isle of Lewis' would sink with the loss of many lives, and that this would occur if a woman wearing red shoes was on board, she being the only survivor. But there was also confusion as to whether this was referring to the ship or the island itself. CalMac described the alarm as 'nonsense', pointing out that the *Isle of Lewis* was seen as the safest ferry for the company yet to sail, and also announced that they would not change her name. In fact there is no such prophecy recorded in Alexander MacKenzie's definitive book, *The Prophesies of the Brahan Seer* and while a witch called *Coinneach Odhar* is documented in Ross-shire at the time, there is very little hard evidence for the Brahan Seer's existence.

On 25 July, the *Isle of Lewis* received last minute work on her bow visor and ramp before leaving Port Glasgow. Her bow and stern ramps, as well as her mezzanine decks, were all hydraulically operated. The bow ramp on the post-Zeebrugge generation of car-ferries, which must remain secure and watertight when closed, even if the bow-visor has been torn away, opens and closes in two stages. It usually took around two to three minutes for the ramp to be fully lowered or raised, and this affected turnaround times. Her stern ramp, which was built as one section, operated in just over a minute. The next day, 26 July, was the day the formal handover of the *Isle of Lewis* was scheduled to take place, and for the new ship to start her delivery voyage to Stornoway.

With all safety concerns resolved, the *Isle of Lewis* finally departed Ferguson's, and indeed Port Glasgow, at 0945 on 26 July, under the command of the late Captain Murdo Kennedy of Kyle of Lochalsh; her first master. Her first task of the day was to carry out lifeboat drills in the Tail of the Bank, and test her drenching system, which she did to the satisfaction of Department of Trade and Industry officials. Next, she cruised into Rothesay Bay to give a couple of 'twirls', positively dwarfing the *Juno* in the process. Finally, she arrived at Ardrossan at 1450, berthing stern-in at the harbour's Irish berth for what, until June 2015, remained her sole visit to the town. She was to take on supplies for her voyage north – including a gangway, several crew cars and stores – and met the *Caledonian Isles* and the *Claymore* during her stay. She was then formally handed over to Caledonian MacBrayne, despite some minor works on her bow outstanding, and departed Ardrossan at 1750, bound for her new home in the Western Isles. Her voyage would see her sail around the south of Mull of Kintyre, through the Sound of Islay, past Colonsay and into the Firth of Lorne past Oban, before turning west through the Sound of Mull and into the Sea of the Hebrides. She would regularly use this path when heading for overhauls on the Clyde or the Mersey in later years.

THREE

The Pride Arrives

Uig Triangle tour and Huge Stornoway Welcome

T HE *ISLE OF LEWIS* was making good progress in the Sea of the Hebrides by the early hours of 27 July, before pausing at Uig, Lochmaddy and Tarbert to undertake berthing trials in order to assess her suitability on the Uig triangle, should an emergency ever arise there in future. As well as using her trials as an opportunity to show herself off to the islanders on Skye, North Uist and Harris, she may also have required the use of either Tarbert or Uig as backup, should her facilities at Stornoway or Ullapool require future maintenance. Almost thirteen hours after leaving Ardrossan, she called first at Uig, from 0630 to 0715, to test her bow ramp only. Next, she sailed across to Lochmaddy, calling there from 0905 to 0955 to test first bow, then stern ramp. Finally, she reached Tarbert, berthing from 1225 to 1250 to test her bow ramp only, after lying off in East Loch Tarbert for a short while waiting for the *Hebridean Isles*, which was using the pier when she arrived, to depart. After completing her trials with relative success, the *Isle of Lewis* left Tarbert, via the Sound of Scalpay – where she had to give way to a yacht in the channel – bound for Ullapool, and then Stornoway to carry out similar trials. On the same day as her tour of the triangle, the Scottish Office Minister Lord James Douglas-Hamilton, on his way to the new ship's inaugural cruise, to take place the following morning, ceremoniously cut the first sod for the new Scalpay Bridge, with the new ship sailing through at that precise moment. Arriving at Ullapool for the first time at 1615, the *Isle of Lewis* tested both her stern ramp and the gangway at the mainland port she would come to know so well, before leaving at 1645 for her new home port.

At 1945, exactly thirty-four hours after leaving Port Glasgow, the *Isle of Lewis* made her first ever arrival into Stornoway, with a 2,000-strong crowd awaiting her, and small boats surrounding her as she entered the harbour. Dressed overall, she slowly edged into No. 1 pier, berthing bow-in to test her bow ramp. Everybody had an opinion on their new vessel, with most very much impressed, especially about her huge size and increased speed compared with the *Suilven*, saying; "The *Isle of Lewis* can go almost as fast backwards as the *Suilven* could forwards." But, there were also some critics who doubted her capabilities, suggesting; "She's ugly compared to the *Suilven*", "She's too high out of the water", while "some ungrateful soul could be heard warning of high winds against the higher-sided ship." Colin Paterson defended his new ship, concluding that such criticism was "completely misplaced", and that she had been "extensively and scientifically tested." New facilities at Newton Basin on the site of the original, long-demolished No. 3 pier were already under way for the *Isle of Lewis*, but they were not ready for her in time; work had only just begun, and she would have to make do with No. 1 pier. The bow visor and ramp took quite some time to fully meet the old linkspan as a result, but following adjustments – achieved with the addition of fat fendering on the pier-face near her stern to help alignment – these were passed off as mere teething-troubles, and she finally landed the ramp onto the linkspan at 2115, one and a half hours after berthing, and was only then able to unload the gangway and cars she took on at Ardrossan. Fifteen minutes later, at 2130, with the *Suilven* approaching, she moved up to the Esplanade berth to allow her predecessor to use the linkspan and unload her last traffic of the day, resulting in new and old ships' first meeting together. She remained there overnight, with the *Suilven* keeping her company for her first night at Stornoway. Although she had not yet entered active service, 27 July 1995 was the busiest day of the *Isle of Lewis*'s career thus far, with five different port calls in that one day thanks to her trial calls at Uig, Lochmaddy, Tarbert, Ullapool and Stornoway. It had been an eventful delivery voyage, and the crew would look forward to a night's rest.

The Press Voyages and *Suilven*'s Last Call

The *Isle of Lewis* undertook a series of special cruises on the Minch prior to entering service. Her main inaugural outing was on the morning of 28 July; the invited guests including Colin Paterson and Lord James Douglas-Hamilton. Unlike the *Suilven*'s stormy maiden voyage in August 1974, the début of the *Isle of Lewis* enjoyed very still waters. After moving from the Esplanade berth to the linkspan at No. 1 pier to load her guests, she departed Stornoway at 0910 on a leisurely sail through the Summer Isles and Loch Broom into Ullapool, where she arrived at 1150 to load more guests and left again at 1215. As she headed back up Loch Broom, she passed the *Suilven* in dramatic style, both vessels exchanging salutes, signifying that a new era was about to begin for the island's shipping services. After lying at Stornoway between 1500 and 1530, the *Isle of Lewis* returned to Ullapool at 1815, remaining there overnight with her bow visor open for a short while as work on the bow ramp continued. Owing to a chess competition being held on Lewis, the *Suilven* was too full to accommodate all the passengers required, and so the *Isle of Lewis* stepped in to help, by taking the extra fifty-two on her afternoon voyage, thus giving her first passenger sailing, although this would not count towards her regular roster.

The next day, 29 July, saw the *Isle of Lewis* leaving Ullapool at 0850, and cruising along the eastern coastline of Lewis before arriving at Stornoway at 1415. She remained at the linkspan until 2030 continuing her bow ramp adjustments, before taking herself on a small sail out to Arnish to allow a dressed *Suilven* to carry out her last ever arrival into Stornoway at 2100 as the sole Lewis ferry, thus bringing her CalMac career to a close. She then immediately handed the service over to the *Isle of Lewis*, scheduled to start her own career on 31 July. On Sunday 30 July, both vessels sat at the pier with the *Isle of Lewis* occupying the linkspan, with her crew continuing work on the bow ramp, with the aim to increase its speed when lowering or rising, as well as finishing painting. The works were carried out at the expense of Ferguson's, and completed successfully. These excursions aside, the public were also invited on board at Stornoway to explore her so that they could familiarise themselves with the new ship before she took up service. Some complaints suggested a lack of seating for parents to supervise their children in the soft play area. However, chief among these complaints was the controversial decision by Colin Paterson not to include sleeping berths, which proved popular on the *Lord of the Isles* on long haul voyages from Oban to the southern islands of the Outer Hebrides, South Uist and Barra. Indeed, the *LOTI* was the last such ship for the company to date to include sleeping accommodation, and as a result – this has been a common occurrence on all vessels – passengers became used to sleeping on the cafeteria seats, the observation lounge or the bar at the stern for night-time sailings.

Getting Down to Business

Once her bow works were completed, the *Isle of Lewis* entered regular service on 31 July 1995 on a brand new roster for the Stornoway ferry, and was again dressed overall for the occasion. As her first day of service was a Monday, she had a full working week with which to begin her career, and the weather was very kind to her, with bright sunshine throughout. Her first commercial sailing left Stornoway at 0200, on time. However, her advertised inaugural sailing of 0810 from Stornoway actually left at 0835, twenty-five minutes late, and she continued to fall behind schedule throughout the remainder of the day. The reason was largely down to her crew's unfamiliarity with the loading arrangements on the massive car deck and, in addition, the difficulty in berthing at the old linkspan in Stornoway. Her passage time had originally been scheduled for two hours thirty minutes, but it was soon found that despite her 18 knot service speed, she actually took ten minutes longer on each crossing. Due to berthing bow-in at Stornoway and stern-in at Ullapool and having to turn out of one port and turn into the other, the outward sail was considered longer than the return. For her first fortnight, the *Isle of Lewis* struggled with her timekeeping; she would finish her day's work anything between 45 minutes to two and a half hours late. However, by mid-August, as the crew became more familiar with the arrangements, the turn-around times were dramatically reduced, and the vessel was able to keep to her schedule more often. One example was on 15 August, when she completed her day's work only eight minutes behind schedule. Despite her tardiness, the new ship became a hit with her passengers with her spacious and modern accommodation, and a delighted Colin Paterson announced that she would, "be a great boost to tourism in the Western Isles and, more importantly, provide a faster luxury service for those who work in the islands."

Suilven Bows Out

Having already stood down from the route on 29 July, the *Suilven* remained at Stornoway for another few days to make sure that the *Isle of Lewis* was able to fully cope on her own, and that there were no other teething troubles for the new ship. Once that was confirmed, the *Suilven* left Stornoway for the final time at 1050 on 4 August to a sentimental send-off from sixty islanders and two pipers. She then called briefly at Lochmaddy to unload her old gangway, which was unsuitable for the *Isle of Lewis*, and a car, before taking on two additional cars and leaving North Uist for her final overhaul in Scottish waters at Troon, arriving there the following morning. She was to be drydocked for propeller work to suit DTI requirements prior to her departure for New Zealand. Once this refit was complete, she was handed over to the Mount Suilven Shipping Company, a subsidiary of Strait Shipping Limited, on 20 August. Three days later, with her funnel repainted light blue, her CalMac legend painted out and her lions removed, the *Suilven* left Troon, and indeed Scotland, for the very last time, sailing via Sheerness for her new career as a livestock transport in New Zealand, arriving at Wellington on 13 October. After nine years of operating between Wellington and Nelson, she moved to Fiji in 2004, and has served there since. Though now on the other side of the world, her seaworthiness became an Internet sensation; a clip of her in the boisterous Cook Strait going viral on YouTube. Sadly, in November 2015, the *Suilven* capsized and sank forty metres below the surface near the entrance to Suva harbour in relatively calm conditions, which was ironically in contrast to her days on the Minch. At the time of writing, a salvage operation is being planned, although the *Suilven* still lies on the seabed near Suva harbour. Despite her slow speed, sparse accommodation and capacity compared to her newer consorts, the *Suilven* had proved herself as a tremendous asset on the Stornoway route for twenty-one years, regularly braving the often tempestuous Minch.

FOUR

The First Few Years

A Great First Season

WITH THE *SUILVEN* now gone, the *Isle of Lewis* was left to operate the service on her own. Her maiden season was a great success, and she became popular with her passengers, who regarded highly her up-to-date and spacious accommodation and faster speed, although she needed time to earn the respect of her illustrious predecessor. Her greater speed and the enhanced roster also saw the start of day trips to Inverness for island shoppers, or to Stornoway for sturdy tourists, and bus services between Inverness and Ullapool had their timetables changed to coincide with the revised schedule. As well as witnessing the new vessel's inauguration, 1995 also saw the opening of the Skye Bridge, which replaced the long-running ferry service from Kyle of Lochalsh to Kyleakin. During the *Isle of Lewis*'s VIP cruise on 28 July, Colin Paterson was asked by Lord James Douglas-Hamilton as to why CalMac were not going to continue the Kyleakin ferry service upon the opening of the bridge. Paterson, quite irritated, is thought to have replied, "It's because you forbade it!"

She became a victim of minor vandalism in late August. As she approached Ullapool, a youth removed one of her fire alarms, creating potential danger to passengers and crew. The 18 year-old apprentice mechanic from Stornoway was fined £300 for the incident at Dingwall Sheriff Court on 17 September. Later in the month, a report in *The Herald* newspaper showed that the berthing fees for the *Isle of Lewis*, which were three times higher than the *Suilven*, had caused fares on the route to rise by 10%. The increase in pier dues was due to the higher gross tonnage of the heavier *Isle of Lewis*, at 6753gt, whereas the *Suilven* was 1908gt. The dispute over pier dues continued for another few years afterwards. The arrival of a new ferry always causes initial traffic problems at the marshalling areas, and barriers were set up to help with this, but the small facilities at King Edward Wharf in Stornoway continued to make traffic management difficult with the *Isle of Lewis*. The Harbour Commission were glad therefore to hear that the new ferry terminal and pier would be ready for April 1997 as planned. Generally, the *Isle of Lewis* performed very well in her maiden season, despite a problem with her turbo-blower on her 0615 sailing to Ullapool on 18 November, which left her stranded there until 1155 the following day. To make matters worse, the relief vessel on the Uig triangle at the time, the *Isle of Arran*, had also broken down, and so both Lewis and Harris were briefly left without any ferry service at all. Occasionally, the *Isle of Lewis* provided 'out of timetable' sailings for the commercial traffic that even she could not accommodate on her passenger sailings, alongside her normal roster. By the time the winter timetable had commenced on 16 October, she had settled down to an official passage time of 2 hours and 45 minutes, and this would stand until the end of her Lewis service.

She then spent her first Christmas dealing with a bizarre incident. On 27 December unprecedentedly low temperatures of around minus 20°C left Stornoway Airport's runway out of action, and the *Isle of Lewis* was chartered by British Airways to take stranded passengers to Ullapool for a bus to Inverness. This gave her a rare chance to prove that she was better than air travel in adverse weather conditions – for once!

Despite her great success in 1995, the *Isle of Lewis* had a problem; loud pounding noises heard at her bow in rough weather, with unsettling vibration. Many began to complain about this and some even fretted over the Brahan Seer's supposed prophecy. Fortunately, this banging was causing no real difficulties for the ship herself. It was traced to her lower bow and underside and in addition, her fendering, the rubber belting on the hull which helps absorb impacts with the pier. The banging arose when she sailed through heavy head-on waves, as her very broad beam made unusual impact. To alleviate the problem she had eight feet of belting, found under the logos denoting the location of the bow thrusters, removed from each side in December 1995, and she managed to handle the Minch better as a result, although the banging and shuddering when stemming heavy seas was never quite eliminated.

Settling in Nicely

1996 was the only full year in which the *Isle of Lewis* used the old linkspan at Stornoway and it was a successful second season for her with little of incident. That November, she went back for her first overhaul to the Garvel drydock. During her refit, she had new covers added on her funnel grills. She was meanwhile relieved at Stornoway by the Oban-Craignure ferry *Isle of Mull*. From 1998 until the end of her service on the route, the *Clansman* assumed the passage in her absence and, from 2006, the *Isle of Lewis* left for her annual serving each January, rather than November. An annual drydocking is a legal requirement for any passenger ship and, an MCA survey apart, allows such maintenance as cleaning of the ship's hull and propellers as cannot be done while she is still afloat. Seaweed and barnacles are removed, anti-fouling paint is applied and the hull itself generally painted. An overhaul besides gives opportunity for major alterations, refurbishment of internal accommodation, and an examination of engines and propulsion. Once the vessel has returned to sea after exiting the dock, she undertakes brief trials and, being satisfied, MCA officials renew her passenger-certificate for another year. On 20 November, after returning to service, the *Isle of Lewis* carried out berthing trials at the new linkspan at Stornoway, berthing first bow-, and then stern-in, with great ease.

In the early hours of 2 February 1997, the *Isle of Lewis* left Stornoway, and together with the *Hebridean Isles* and the Stornoway lifeboat, she undertook exercises in stormy seas off the Butt of Lewis, in a charter to the Norwegian company Selantic. They were testing a newly developed evacuation system which had been installed, and wanted to assess its performance in adverse weather. The *Isle of Lewis* played the ship in distress, as she had the equipment installed, with the *Hebridean Isles* and the Stornoway lifeboat doubling up as the recovery vessels. Unfortunately, the system required a minimum of Force 6 conditions and a reasonably heavy swell in order to be tested properly, and as the weather was not extreme enough, the exercise had to be abandoned, and the two ferries soon returned to their respective routes. Two months later, on 2 April, the *Isle of Lewis* herself became a rescue vessel, assisting a small fishing boat, the *Kaywye*, in distress in Loch Broom. The *Isle of Lewis* stood by her for about two hours until the arrival of the lifeboat from Portree, Skye. On 24 April, the *Isle of Lewis* carried out further trials at her new, almost complete Stornoway pier.

New Facilities Open at Stornoway

Four days later, on 28 April 1997, the new Stornoway facilities were open for use and the *Isle of Lewis* found berthing in Stornoway much easier as a result. The terminal building took its design from the former fish market, demolished in 1970 when the *Loch Seaforth* was still operating the Kyle/Mallaig mailboat run. A wind vane, designed by steeplejack Fred Dibnah, was installed on top of the terminal building. In addition, a large marshalling area of seven lanes was installed, with the seventh lane being for buses picking up or setting down passengers from the ship. On 14 May, James Shaw Grant officially opened the new facilities and the *Isle of Lewis* was dressed overall to celebrate the occasion, with bunting also put up around the terminal. Now that the *Isle of Lewis* had two Stornoway terminals available to her in the event of breakdown, she no longer required the use of Tarbert as back-up, and she did not return to the Harris terminal until June 2015.

During her second overhaul at the Garvel drydock in November 1997, the *Isle of Lewis* had her cylinder heads renewed and also received a new bow ramp in order to comply with more upgrades to SOLAS. The new ramp was the same shape as before, and was also installed with two orange barriers on each side to avoid people falling overboard. They would be folded up just before the ramp was ready to close, and put into its stowed-away position when the bow visor was raised or ready to lower. After her refit, the *Isle of Lewis* called at CalMac HQ in Gourock for the first time for trials, both bow- and stern-in, so that she could discharge or load crew cars during future overhauls on the Clyde. Her off-centre ramps sat on the linkspan with great success.

Major Breakdown

In 1998, the *Isle of Lewis* was called, on two occasions, to operate special sailings to and from Lochmaddy, carrying vehicles for the Ministry of Defence during heavy army movements that spring. These charters relieved the pressure on the *Hebridean Isles*, the then-regular vessel on the Uig triangle. The *Isle of Lewis*'s successful bow and stern trials at Lochmaddy in 1995 made her quite suitable for this unique role. Other vessels which helped with assistance in carrying military vehicles were the *Isle of Mull* and the *Pioneer*.

It was during the first of these charters, however, that the *Isle of Lewis* suddenly came to a grinding halt, and, considering her cargo that morning, gave an impression of a Dad's Army-style calamity. In the early hours of 19 April 1998, after arriving at Lochmaddy at 0330 from Ullapool and unloading her vehicles, she was attempting to leave in order to return to Stornoway, when her port engine seized, and she was forced to berth again to allow examinations to be carried out. It was discovered that there was a defect in the alignment in both propeller shafts, both of which existed from her construction, and due to this, the 'A' bracket bearing in the port shaft had failed, causing the sudden stoppage of the port engine. As this issue could not be corrected whilst she was still in the water, the *Isle of Lewis* was forced to limp on one engine from Lochmaddy, which she departed from at 0810, to the Garvel drydock in Greenock, arriving on 20 April. The *Isle of Mull* was immediately summoned from Oban to cover the Stornoway service. At Oban, the *Pioneer* took over the *Isle of Mull*'s usual roster, and was joined by the *Pentalina B* (ex *Iona*), sold in 1997, but chartered back to assist the *Pioneer* at Oban. These problems caused severe headaches for CalMac as they lacked a proper backup ship. The *Claymore* had also been sold in 1996, and the *Iona*'s departure from the fleet in 1997 was due to her inability to meet further developments for SOLAS. The problems were compounded by the late arrival of the *Clansman*, the new Oban-based vessel that was to replace the *Lord of the Isles*, which eventually entered service in July 1998. She also became the major winter relief vessel.

On 14 May, the *Isle of Lewis* returned to service four days earlier than expected, much to everyone's surprise, thus demonstrating her resilience.

On 31 May, she made an unscheduled second visit to Lochmaddy, problem-free this time around, and was called on to carry more army vehicles and a Barratlantic lorry to Ullapool, which as it turned out, was actually closer to the traffic's ultimate destination than Uig would have been.

Tyne Overhaul and Orkney Visit

In November, she visited Wallsend on the Tyne for her annual overhaul, making CalMac history at the same time, becoming the company's first vessel under usual circumstances to be overhauled outside of Scotland, although the *Isle of Mull* had been lengthened at Middlesbrough at the end of her first season in 1988. The *Isle of Lewis* spent the next three weeks undergoing her refit, before leaving for Stornoway on 26 November, despite having to call into Aberdeen the following day to rectify engine trouble experienced *en route*.

On 28 November, the *Isle of Lewis* made a historic visit to Stromness in Orkney to 'show the flag' during the bidding process for the Northern Isles franchise. The Northern Isles routes from Aberdeen and Stromness had been operated at the time by P&O, and CalMac was actually one of the potential bidders for the services when they went out to tender. This visit to Stromness was part of the *Isle of Lewis*'s duty as CalMac's then-flagship to demonstrate the company's interest in the Orkney and Shetland routes, and she was berthed from 0900 until 1335. The exercise was a huge success, with almost 700 Orcadians going aboard. It would be another four years until the arrival of NorthLink, the operators in the Northern Isles from 2002. From 2012, they began trading under the name Serco NorthLink, as the David MacBrayne Group lost the tender to the controversial Hampshire-based outsourcing company. NorthLink's vessels included the *Hrossey* and the *Hjaltland*, both operating from Aberdeen to Lerwick in Shetland, with one sailing via Kirkwall, Orkney, and the *Hamnavoe*, which operated from Scrabster to Stromness across the Pentland Firth, another crossing known for its tempestuous conditions. All three ships were built at Aker Finnyards in Finland, with Ferguson's of Port Glasgow originally tendering for the contract of the *Hamnavoe*. It could be said that the *Isle of Lewis* influenced the design of each NorthLink vessel. She returned to service at Stornoway and enjoyed a satisfactory end to 1998, which had undoubtedly been one of the most eventful seasons of her career. It was the *Clansman*'s turn to show the flag in Stromness in 2000, exactly as the *Isle of Lewis* had done two years previously.

A New Century Begins

The *Isle of Lewis* had two successful years before the close of the Second Millennium, and continued to go about her daily business crossing the Minch. On 17 February 1999, she was involved in a rescue mission in poor visibility twenty minutes into her afternoon return trip to Stornoway. A flare had been seen, and in response, the *Isle of Lewis* conducted a search, and the crew found a man wearing a lifejacket in heavy seas close to wreckage. She remained by the man's side until a fishing boat rescued him, before continuing to Stornoway once again. On 5 September, she went out north of the Butt of Lewis on trials to investigate vibration problems. She had apparently developed shudders which passengers became quite worried about, but nobody could determine the cause of the shuddering. A surveyor was on board the *Isle of Lewis* off the Butt from 1400 to 2200. The vessel had to cancel her early morning return trip to Ullapool due to the crew's legal rest periods. In the end, it was concluded that the ship was fine, and that the shuddering was 'natural'; it would remain with her for the rest of her working life. In November, during her second visit to Wallsend for overhaul, she received a new Fast Rescue Craft and framework on her port deck aft of the bridge.

The 2000 season, the first of the Third Millennium, was rather uneventful. In May, she had to return to the former No. 1 pier at Stornoway for around two weeks while essential repairs were carried out at No. 3 pier. Occasional high tide meant that passengers had to walk off through the car deck, as the gangway at the old pier was too steep in the circumstances. In November, she returned once again to Wallsend for her overhaul. 2000 was also the *Isle of Lewis*'s final full year as CalMac flagship, being succeeded by her 'shipyard sister', the *Hebrides*, which replaced the *Hebridean Isles* on the Uig triangle in March 2001. I use the unusual term 'shipyard sister' because the *Isle of Lewis* and the *Hebrides* were both built by Ferguson's of Port Glasgow, and launched within five years of each other.

FIVE

Competition on the Minch

T HE 2001 SEASON was dominated by a controversial freight war. Although the *Isle of Lewis* was large enough to accommodate all the commercial traffic demanding shipment to and from Stornoway, she began to struggle with the ever-increasing volume of it in her daily passenger sailings. The first vessel to provide competition with commercial traffic was the *Highland Carrier* in 1998, a container vessel which provided a service from Stornoway to Kyle of Lochalsh, as she could not use the linkspan at Ullapool. By early 2001, the next competing ship arrived in the shape of the *White Sea*. She was a thirty-six year old stern-loading vessel built in Norway, chartered by Aberdeen-based Taygran Shipping, and used on the route from March until May. Despite being an old, slow and unreliable vessel, she did make serious inroads into CalMac's trade, but CalMac were quick to respond to the threat of losing the service to the competition. Replacing the *White Sea* in May was a more useful vessel, the *Taygran Trader*, a navy-hulled ro-ro loading vessel with bow and stern loading features, originally owned by P&O as the *European Trader*. Although the *Isle of Lewis* found free space for daily tourist traffic thanks to the competition, she still found herself carrying a majority of freight, as some island hauliers were not entirely convinced by Taygran's agenda. They continued using the more trustworthy *Isle of Lewis*, although CalMac reported a 12.9% decrease in commercial traffic for June 2001, itself a result of the higher competition from Taygran. However, a report for the same month showed a rise of 2.4% for passengers, 5.5% for cars and 11.9% for coaches, and this gave CalMac some reassurance.

However, on 30 August, because of financial troubles which included unpaid pier dues to Stornoway Pier & Harbour Commission, it was announced that Taygran Shipping had gone into receivership, and the *Taygran Trader* remained stranded at Stornoway pier. The ship herself had been arrested on 7 August, after an incident in which she failed to return to Stornoway, and it fell to the *Isle of Lewis* to save the day. A writ was tied to the *Taygran Trader*'s mast to signify the arrest, and unpaid debts to the Pier & Harbour Commission in Stornoway. She was later refitted and sold for further service in Egypt. The *Taygran Trader*'s eventual departure from Stornoway handed the overnight service to the *Isle of Lewis*, thus winning the battle against Taygran Shipping and taking over the night service along with her regular daily roster. She commenced this on 9 August on an 'ad-hoc' basis, and then from 13 August permanently. However, because of crew considerations, the service became difficult to sustain.

As an alternative, it was realised that a second vessel could be used on the overnight sailing, and that this would relieve the pressures that the *Isle of Lewis* was experiencing. The benefit of this service was that the majority of commercial vehicles could be accommodated on the second vessel through the night, and that there would then be sufficient space for tourist traffic on the *Isle of Lewis* during the day. Another benefit of the overnight service would be that island shoppers would be able to buy the same items at the same price and time of day as those on the mainland. So, the *Lord of the Isles* – and subsequently the *Isle of Arran* – began a second roster on the route in order to help their fleet mate out with the commercial traffic. Although there had been rumours that the *Isle of Arran* had been brought to Stornoway to replace the *Isle of Lewis*, the former Arran ferry was only visiting to carry out berthing trials there and at Ullapool when she called on 12 March. As with the competing ships, the *Isle of Arran* shared the roster with the *Isle of Lewis*, and one ship had to use No. 1 pier in Stornoway if No. 3 was occupied by the other vessel, or *vice versa*. Eventually, the *Isle of Arran* was released, and the NorthLink ferry *Hascosay* took over as a stop gap between May and September 2002 before she was ready for service in the Northern Isles routes from Aberdeen; NorthLink having taken over the services from P&O that year.

Finally, a permanent vessel was found in the shape of the *Belard*, formerly of P&O; she had sailed between Ardrossan and Belfast, hence her name. When she first arrived in Stornoway in September 2002, her owners were Harrison's (Clyde) Limited. Renamed the *Mùirneag*, she entered service with CalMac lions and the company protocol painted on her funnels and superstructure, but her hull remained blue to signify that she was under charter. Despite being a seaworthy vessel, she was unflatteringly referred to by locals as the 'Olympic Flame' (which never went out!), owing to the poor sea conditions in the Minch which prevented her from sailing. She also had occasional manoeuvrability issues when berthing in Stornoway, as local commercial traffic was too light for her and left her stern very high out of the water. As for the *Isle of Lewis*, she had returned again to Wallsend for overhaul in November 2001 for the fifth time in four years, but this was to be, to date, her final visit there. She was on the Tyne between 12 November and 3 December, and was surveyed in separate docks during that period. The Gaelic version of her name and the company protocol were painted in between the windows on the superstructure near the bow on both sides, as a result of the 2001/02 CalMac policy for all vessels in the fleet to feature their bilingual names on their hulls and superstructure.

Six

An Unlikely Duo

A Return to Normality

ONCE THE *MÙIRNEAG* had settled into her new routine, Lewis had a satisfactory service from her and the *Isle of Lewis* for the next decade. All the pressures that affected the *Isle of Lewis* had simply evaporated, and there was an incident-free service from the two vessels. During an overhaul in Aberdeen in November 2002, the *Isle of Lewis*, like all of her fleetmates, had the company protocol repainted in red and black on the superstructure below the funnels, and her Gaelic name *Eilean Leodhais* repainted in black in between the front windows on each side of the bow. Nothing eventful occurred until March 2003, when she hit the pier at Ullapool with great force, resulting in major damage to the port side of her stern. This accident caused her to be withdrawn and the *Clansman* had to take over while she found sanctuary at Aberdeen to repair the damage to her stern. In November, she arrived in the A&P drydock in Birkenhead, Liverpool, for her annual overhaul, this being her first of many visits there. Pictures taken of this overhaul were featured in a large frame on board the ship's main entrance concourse. She returned to Stornoway nearly three weeks later on the 21st, once again taking the service back from the *Clansman*.

The 2004 season ran without problem. The *Clansman* returned to the fray over the New Year to relieve the *Mùirneag* for her overhaul. On 15 October, the *Isle of Lewis* was the unusual venue for a wedding ceremony on board shortly after her afternoon arrival in Stornoway. This very romantic occasion delayed her next departure to Ullapool by about half an hour. In November, she returned to Birkenhead for overhaul. This time, she had a major internal refurbishment for the first time in her nine-year service, with the promise of more disabled and child-friendly facilities. One of the main changes was the conversion of the TV Lounge into a family room which incorporated children's arcade games and soft play area, as well as seats and a large LCD television. The original soft play area on Deck 4 was converted into an 18+ amusement games room. A great deal of carpeting around the vessel was upgraded too, as was the seating in the dog areas. Disabled access to the cafeteria was also upgraded. More LCD TV screens, along with improved coffee and snack facilities, were installed in the bar. CalMac decided not to make public details about the expense of these refurbishments, however. The *Isle of Lewis* left Birkenhead on 15 November following trials, passing off the eastern coast of Scalpay during her return to Stornoway, taking the service over from the *Clansman* again on 17 November.

Just before Christmas, the *Isle of Lewis* came to the rescue to take 'Santa Claus' and his reindeer to Stornoway, in a humorous festive gesture from CalMac. 'Santa' had been due to attend a Christmas fair on the island, but because 'reindeers only fly on Christmas Eve', the *Isle of Lewis* became Noah's Ark, so that she could bring them to Stornoway in time for the fair.

SEVEN

A Decade On

In the 2005 season, the *Isle of Lewis* celebrated ten years of service on the Stornoway-Ullapool route. It did not start too well however, when the entire CalMac network was shut down on 11 January, as hurricane force winds of over 100mph risked destruction to the whole west coast of Scotland. On 10 November, she suffered a breakdown which left her out of service for nearly a week, being replaced once again by the *Clansman*. Things were further exacerbated on 11 November, when the *Mùirneag* sailed from Ullapool in a major storm, and was stuck in the Minch for sixteen hours. This ordeal resulted in passengers injured and a vintage car being seriously damaged. The injured passengers were treated at the Western Isles Hospital in Stornoway, and voiced their criticism of the master's decision to sail in such conditions, with one apparently saying, "I thought I was going to die." Fortunately for the *Isle of Lewis*, she was still awaiting repairs for her breakdown, and so avoided the storm. Once repaired, she ended the 2005 season without further problems, and was due, once again, to undertake her annual overhaul at Birkenhead in February 2006. This was changed from the usual time of November, owing to the fact that she had not had an overhaul in 2004.

First Visit to Oban

The *Isle of Lewis* began 2006 with no problems. On 28 January, the *Clansman* took over the Stornoway service from her. She then sailed straight to Birkenhead, arriving at 0015 on 30 January, and her overhaul began later that morning. During the refit, she received refurbishments to her catering area in the cafeteria, and also had her outdated Racal Decca radar system, with which she had been built, replaced with the more modern Sperry Marine system, which included thinner radar scanners, and has become standard equipment on many fleet members. Meanwhile, the *Clansman* was doing an excellent job in her role as relief ship at Stornoway, constantly running to timetable and making sure that all traffic was catered for on all sailings. The *Isle of Lewis* completed her overhaul and departed Birkenhead on the evening of 17 February and headed back north to resume service. During her return, she made her first ever call at Oban. Shortly after the *Isle of Mull*'s 0800 departure to Craignure, the *Isle of Lewis* berthed stern-in at the linkspan for bunkering, and also undertook tests with the old gangway. Because her stern ramp was not off-set to starboard to suit the Oban linkspan, she did not test it. After leaving Oban at 0930, she continued onto Stornoway, and passed through the Sound of Mull, meeting the *Isle of Arran* and the *Isle of Cumbrae* near Tobermory, Mull. The *Isle of Cumbrae* was relieving on the Tobermory-Kilchoan service, usually served by the Loch Class vessel, the *Loch Linnhe*.

The rest of the 2006 season for the *Isle of Lewis* ran like clockwork, and she put in another good performance, with only weather disruptions holding her back, as is the case with every year, and every other vessel. Worthy of mentioning is that from the period of early September to June, the *Isle of Lewis* would normally perform two daily return sailings, at the same times every day. During the summer months, she would bring her first two return sailings forward an hour on certain days of the week – most recently on Wednesdays and Fridays – and perform a third return sailing in the late evening, not returning to Stornoway until the early hours of the following morning. This was the case throughout her duration on the service.

One major change that affected the *Isle of Lewis*, and all vessels in the fleet for that matter, was the division, on 1 October 2006, of Caledonian MacBrayne Ltd into two separate companies, in order to comply with new European Union guidelines on State Aids in Maritime Transport. The first company was Caledonian Maritime Assets Limited (CMAL), an asset-owning company wholly owned by the Scottish Government, and which was basically Caledonian MacBrayne renamed. It took ownership

Loch Seaforth approaching Kyle of Lochalsh, 1957.
(*Andrew Clark, CRSC*)

Suilven passing a jet skier as she approaches Stornoway, 26 July 1995.
(*Michael MacLennan*)

Isle of Lewis **under construction at Ferguson's, February 1995.**
(*Jim Aikman Smith*)

Isle of Lewis **is launched, 18 April 1995.**
(*Graham Todd*)

Isle of Lewis fitting out at Port Glasgow, July 1995.
(*Jim Aikman Smith*)

Isle of Lewis and *Juno* in Rothesay Bay, 26 July 1995.
(*Ian MacLagan*)

Isle of Lewis meets *Caledonian Isles* at Ardrossan, 26 July 1995.
(*David Stirling*)

Isle of Lewis approaching Uig, Skye for trials, 27 July 1995.
(*Isla MacEwan*)

Isle of Lewis at Lochmaddy for trials, 27 July 1995.
(*Iain McPherson*)

Isle of Lewis at Tarbert, Harris for trials, 27 July 1995.
(*Jim Aikman Smith*)

Isle of Lewis arrives in Stornoway for the first time, 27 July 1995.
(*Jack Kernahan*)

Isle of Lewis meets *Suilven* for the first time, 27 July 1995.
(*Michael MacLennan*)

Isle of Lewis in Ullapool on her VIP cruise, 28 July 1995.
(*Chris Williams*)

Suilven's last ever arrival into Stornoway, 29 July 1995.
(*Michael MacLennan*)

Isle of Lewis having bow ramp adjustments made at Stornoway, 30 July 1995. (*Jim Aikman Smith*)

Isle of Lewis leaving Stornoway on her first day of service, 31 July 1995. (*Jim Aikman Smith*)

Suilven leaves Stornoway for the final time, 4 August 1995.
(*Michael MacLennan*)

Isle of Lewis leaves Stornoway, 14 August 1995.
(*Michael MacLennan*)

Isle of Lewis bow-in at Ullapool, August 1995.
(*Hugh Smith*)

Isle of Lewis arriving in Stornoway, 19 September 1996.
(*Michael MacLennan*)

Isle of Lewis's first overhaul on the Clyde, 17 November 1996.
(*Lawrence Macduff*)

Isle of Lewis's berthing trials at No. 3 pier, Stornoway,
20 November 1996. (*Michael MacLennan*)

Isle of Lewis and *Hebridean Isles* in Stornoway together,
27 January 1997. (*Michael MacLennan*)

Isle of Lewis in a storm off the Butt of Lewis, 2 February 1997.
(*John Horne*)

Isle of Lewis at the official opening of the ferry terminal in
Stornoway, 14 May 1997. (*Angus Smith Photographic*)

Isle of Lewis in drydock at Wallsend, November 1998.
(*John Park*)

Isle of Lewis leaves the Tyne, 26 November 1998.
(*Kevin Blair*)

Isle of Lewis leaving Stromness, Orkney after 'showing the flag',
28 November 1998. (*Willie Mackay*)

Highland Carrier entering Stornoway, 9 November 1998.
(*Michael MacLennan*)

Isle of Lewis and *White Sea* in Stornoway, 8 March 2001.
(*Michael MacLennan*)

Isle of Lewis and *Taygran Trader* at Stornoway, 2001.
(*Jack Kernahan*)

Isle of Lewis and *Lord of the Isles*, November 2001.
(*Jack Kernahan*)

Isle of Lewis passes *Isle of Arran* off Stornoway, 2002.
(*Jack Kernahan*)

Isle of Lewis and *Hascosay* at Stornoway, 2002.
(*Jack Kernahan*)

Isle of Lewis and *Muirneag* at Stornoway, 2006.
(*Jack Kernahan*)

Isle of Mull at Stornoway, 1 December 1997, relieving *Isle of Lewis*.
(*Michael MacLennan*)

Isle of Lewis and *Clansman* at Stornoway, 29 December 2009.
(*Jack Kernahan*)

Isle of Lewis leaving Aberdeen, 30 March 2003.
(*David Sinclair*)

Isle of Lewis and *Muirneag* at No. 3 pier, Stornoway, 2004.
(*Jack Kernahan*)

Isle of Lewis celebrates her 10th birthday in Ullapool, 2005.
(*Neil Hamilton*)

Isle of Lewis leaving Oban for Castlebay, 30 August 2015.
(*Stuart Mackillop*)

Isle of Lewis at Brodick, Arran for trials, 7 June 2015.
(*Stuart Mackillop*)

Isle of Lewis and *Hebridean Princess* at Stornoway, 29 July 2006.
(*Jack Kernahan*)

Isle of Lewis approaching Ullapool, 2007.
(*Dave Wolstenholme*)

Isle of Lewis meets *Jupiter* off Gourock, 6 January 2008.
(*John Crae*)

Isle of Lewis meets *Loch Alainn* at Gourock, 6 January 2008.
(*John Newth*)

Isle of Lewis squeezing past *Coruisk* on entry into James Watt Dock,
6 January 2008. (*John Newth*)

Isle of Lewis with *Loch Shira* at James Watt Dock, 22 January 2008.
(*John Crae*)

Isle of Lewis with *Pentalina-B (Iona)* in Stornoway, November 2008.
(*Jack Kernahan*)

Isle of Lewis in Frederica, Denmark, 8 February 2009.
(*Jesper Andersen, jtashipphoto.dk*)

Isle of Lewis meets *Queen Mary 2* mid-Minch, 18 October 2009.
(*John Horne*)

Isle of Lewis leaves Greenock with her new funnel additions,
8 February 2010. (*John Newth*)

Isle of Lewis in Ullapool with Lawrence Macduff's
MacBrayne's bus, 2011. (*Lawrence Macduff*)

Isle of Lewis leaves Stornoway, 2011.
(*Lawrence Macduff*)

Isle of Lewis meets *Britannia* at Leith, 13 February 2013.
(*Gordon Stirling*)

Isle of Lewis meets *Hebrides* in Stornoway, 15 February 2013.
(*Mark Nicolson*)

Muirneag and *Isle of Lewis* at Stornoway, 29 September 2013.
(*Mark Nicolson*)

Isle of Lewis enters Garvel drydock, 6 October 2013.
(*Stuart Mackillop*)

Isle of Lewis meets *Hallaig* off Inverkip, 10 October 2013.
(*Stuart Mackillop*)

Isle of Lewis meets *Clipper Ranger* off Stornoway, 30 May 2014.
(*Mark Nicolson*)

Clansman and *Hebridean Isles* at Stornoway, 7 February 2014.
(*Mark Nicolson*)

Isle of Lewis in Birkenhead, 2 March 2014.
(*Andy Mahon*)

Isle of Lewis and *Clipper Ranger* at Stornoway, 24 July 2014.
(*Mark Nicolson*)

Isle of Lewis meets *Black Watch* as she leaves Stornoway,
26 August 2014. (*Mark Nicolson*)

Loch Seaforth leaving Stornoway, 24 February 2015.
(*Mark Nicolson*)

Isle of Lewis at Castlebay, Barra on trials, 5 June 2015.
(*John Macdougall*)

Isle of Lewis and *Suilven* in Stornoway, 30 July 1995.
(*Michael MacLennan*)

Isle of Lewis meets *Loch Seaforth* at Stornoway, 20 March 2015.
(*Mark Nicolson*)

Isle of Lewis leaves Tarbert, Harris in original condition,
27 July 1995. (*Kenny MacAskill*)

Isle of Lewis's cafeteria, July 1995.
(*John Newth*)

Isle of Lewis's lounge bar, 3 September 2014.
(*Mark Nicolson*)

Isle of Lewis's main entrance concourse, 3 September 2014.
(*Mark Nicolson*)

Isle of Lewis's observation lounge, 8 July 2004.
(*Lawrence Macduff*)

Isle of Lewis's TV lounge, 3 September 2014.
(*Mark Nicolson*)

Isle of Lewis's car deck, 3 September 2014.
(*Mark Nicolson*)

Isle of Lewis's starboard Mirrlees Blackstone K6 Major
diesel engine, 4 April 2014. (*Mark Nicolson*)

Isle of Lewis's bridge.
(*Niall Sinclair*)

Isle of Lewis's open deck, July 1995.
(*Jack Kernahan*)

Captain Alex Morrison

Captain Lewis Mackenzie

of all vessels and terminals owned by CalMac. The second company was CalMac Ferries Limited, a subsidiary of the David MacBrayne Group and an operating company which took over the operation of all the routes after they were put out to tender, commencing a six year contract on 1 October 2007. Throughout January and February 2007, the *Isle of Lewis* was at Birkenhead for her overhaul for the fourth time in five years. 2007 was another successful season for her and she ran without trouble, with no breakdowns being recorded for the year.

Coming of Age

Return to the Clyde for Overhaul

THE 2008 SEASON, however, saw the *Isle of Lewis* deviate from her Birkenhead overhaul schedule, and she made her first visit to the Garvel drydock in Greenock since May 1998, where she underwent repairs following the major breakdown she suffered at Lochmaddy. When she arrived at Gourock at 1435 on 6 January to unload crew cars, she met the *Loch Alainn* sitting at the 'wires' awaiting a spell of relief duty on the Cumbrae service in place of the *Loch Shira*, which would later join the *Isle of Lewis* at the Garvel. On entry into the James Watt Dock, the *Isle of Lewis* had to squeeze past the *Coruisk*, another vessel undergoing her overhaul. In drydock, she had major changes made to her observation lounge, and partitions were installed in the seating, following complaints that sleeping passengers were taking up too much space. Glass panels were installed to help reduce noise levels from the children's play area. These improvements totalled £165,000. The vessel returned to Stornoway through adverse weather under the command of Captain Alex Morrison, who, having first joined her in 1997, was the master most associated with her. On 25 July, the *Mùirneag* had suffered a steering gear failure and had run aground close to the Lews Castle Grounds. The *Isle of Lewis* took over the freight service whilst the *Mùirneag* went to Aberdeen to check for damage, with none being found. The *Isle of Lewis* thus resumed her duties on 31 July; the thirteenth anniversary of her maiden voyage, but things did not go well, as she suffered a failure to the port-side mezzanine deck, resulting in difficulties in accommodating all the required traffic.

In November, the Ullapool linkspan was out of action for a week so that essential maintenance could be carried out. The *Isle of Lewis* thus provided passenger-only services between Stornoway and Ullapool, whereas freight had to arrive from Uig, Skye. She gave only two sailings per day for that week; the 0715 to Ullapool in the morning, and then the 1715 back to Stornoway. As the *Mùirneag* was away in Wallsend for overhaul, she was replaced by the *Pentalina B*, which was chartered back to CalMac for the first time in ten years, and she sailed between Stornoway and Uig on the freight roster. On 11 November, the *Isle of Lewis* took advantage of the high tide at Skye to make her second ever call at Uig. This visit took place in between her passenger sailings, and she was to collect freight traffic that could not be catered for by the *Pentalina B*, as she was stormbound in Stornoway. The *Isle of Lewis* was at Uig from 1450 to 1510 taking on the freight, before returning to Ullapool to carry out her second passenger sailing of the day, and she departed Ullapool for Stornoway at 1815 (for 1715), carrying both passengers and the freight she collected at Uig earlier. The Ullapool linkspan re-opened on 17 November, and vehicle services returned to normal. In late December, the *Isle of Lewis* was joined by the *Lord of the Isles*, which took over the freight run from the *Pentalina B* until the *Mùirneag* was ready to return from the Tyne. The *Pentalina B*'s charter to CalMac had run its intended course; hence the reason for the *LOTI*'s arrival in Stornoway.

The *Isle of Lewis* makes History ... on a Sunday

At the beginning of the 2009 season the *Isle of Lewis* was looking much the worse for wear as she approached her annual refit – one window on the starboard side having been boarded up – but her overhaul would soon refresh her again. At the end of January, she was booked into the Frederica drydock in Denmark, making her the first CalMac ship to be overhauled outside the United Kingdom. She was also intended to be the third major vessel, along with the *Hebrides* in 2007, and the *Clansman* in 2008, to be converted to burn Intermediate Fuel Oil as a less expensive alternative to Marine Diesel Oil. She returned to service after a small lay-up in Ullapool. A common concern of the IFO fuel was that she produced unpleasant amounts of thick black smoke from her funnels prior to every departure, and CalMac were in danger of being prosecuted under pollution laws because of this. It has to be said that this change in fuel would have a significant impact on the *Isle of Lewis*'s mechanical performance over the next few years.

Sunday sailings to Stornoway have always been a controversial subject, despite the majority of islanders campaigning for them. They had already been introduced across the Sound of Harris in April 2006, so it was no wonder that so many wished for them to be introduced at Stornoway also. On 14 July 2009, CalMac announced that the *Isle of Lewis* would start regular sailings to Ullapool on a Sunday, and the first of these would take place at 1430 on 19 July. However, on 17 July, during her 1025 sailing from Ullapool, she suffered an exhaust failure in her starboard engine. After unloading her traffic, she remained at Stornoway undergoing repairs, and was replaced by the *Isle of Arran*. The breakdown was claimed by traditionalists to be an 'act of God', when in reality, it was simply a pure mechanical issue. The *Isle of Lewis* was repaired the following evening, and wasted no time in catching up with the sailings she had missed. The *Isle of Arran* arrived in Stornoway in the early hours of the 19th, unintentionally becoming the first ferry to sail into the town on the Sabbath. However, this did not matter, as the *Isle of Lewis* was ready to undertake the very first scheduled Sunday sailing over the Minch that afternoon at 1430. Oblivious to protests from parishioners, the vessel was given a raucous send-off from locals as she departed for Ullapool. Police were present at both terminals to control protesters. Every Sunday from 19 July until the end of her Stornoway service, the *Isle of Lewis* made one timetabled return sailing – leaving Stornoway at 1430, and Ullapool at 1815.

Difficult Times

The 2010 season began with the *Isle of Lewis* trying to regain form after a year of breakdowns in 2009. As a result of the change to a heavier fuel grade, the level of thick black smoke emitting from her funnels was deemed unacceptable, and so during her overhaul in the Garvel in January, she had new silver exhaust uptakes installed in the top of her funnels to help reduce the amount of smoke which was making the open deck dirty, and also to make sure it was emitting completely upright. On 10 April, she broke down again and people vented their anger in an online campaign to 'Replace MV *Isle of Lewis*', where derogatory comments about the vessel were made, exaggeratingly claiming that she had always been dogged with problems. The campaign also made disparaging comparisons of the ship to her predecessor, the *Suilven*. This did not show the locals in the best light, with their demands for another new vessel in less than twenty years. A petition to CalMac to remove the *Isle of Lewis* from the route was also up for consideration, but this did not happen, and the online campaign was later terminated.

In July it was announced that there were plans to replace both ships with a new single vessel, which would be faster and much larger. However, the idea of a single replacement was not enthusiastically welcomed, and for very good reasons. Instead, there was an argument for a dual ship service of vessels similar in size to the *Isle of Lewis* performing a shuttle service across the Minch – as was the case on routes such as Wemyss Bay-Rothesay with the *Bute* and the *Argyle* – and that this would offer a better level of frequency on the route. However, the shipping experts maintained that a dual ship service would be too expensive to operate. Meanwhile the *Isle of Lewis* redeemed herself by having a very successful summer in 2010, rarely missing a sailing during the period of the Hebridean Celtic Festival, and this saved her reputation for a time. On 23 July she had a visitor, in the shape of the *Hebridean Princess*, which was carrying Queen Elizabeth II on her Scottish island cruise, and ferry passengers leaving on the afternoon sailing to Ullapool that day were able to see the Queen disembarking. The last time Her Majesty had visited Stornoway was on 29 July 2006, during her 80th birthday celebrations, when the *Isle of Lewis* had been dressed overall to show her appreciation of the monarch. She ended 2010 on a damp patch, however, suffering a turbocharger failure on Hogmanay, and she was replaced by the *Lord of the Isles*. She had to sail to Ullapool on 4 January 2011 on one engine to have repairs carried out, and resumed service the following day.

A Better Year

2011 was a better year for the *Isle of Lewis* with fewer breakdowns than 2010. On 30 January, she returned to Birkenhead for her overhaul for the first time since 2007. On 16 February, she made her second visit to Oban, between 1210 and 1305, for bunkering during her return voyage north, and the *Clansman* once again handed the Stornoway service back to her.

On 16 March, Caledonian Maritime Assets Limited held a meeting in Stornoway Town Hall to discuss the future of the Stornoway-Ullapool route, and asked people to voice their opinion on what kind of service they wanted. The *Mùirneag* was due to retire from service in October 2013, the date CMAL hoped they would have a replacement ship in service for both vessels. Various options were listed, and given the recent misfortunes suffered by the *Isle of Lewis*, an option which involved retaining her on the route as the sole vessel with an enhanced timetable was abruptly, and quite rightly rejected. Other options included having her teamed up with a new vessel of similar size, fully replacing her with a much larger purpose-built ship capable of 24 hour operation, or build two new vessels, similar in size to the *Clansman* and the *Hebrides*, to perform a shuttle service, this offering the best frequency. CMAL also showed a list of capacity and reliability statistics up to that moment, and exhibited computer-generated previews of the proposed replacement vessel, to carry 143 cars/20 HGVs and 600 to 700 passengers. They also gave her dimensions and benefits compared to the *Isle of Lewis*. It would be another year before CMAL would officially announce their final option; to repeat the events of July 1995, and commission a new purpose-built single vessel replacement on the route by summer 2014. The *Isle of Lewis* continued her usual duties, taking concerns about her future in her stride. On 18 June, she was slightly delayed leaving Stornoway when her bow visor locked, but on the whole, 2011 was an improvement over 2010.

NINE

Questions Needed Answering

WITH TALK OF AN APOCALYPSE in 2012, the world certainly felt as if it ending for the *Isle of Lewis*. She had the first of two of her worst performing seasons in her career, and it seemed that the decision to convert her to use IFO fuel should have had serious second thoughts. The year started well until she went to Birkenhead for overhaul, with the *Clansman*, as usual, taking her place at Stornoway. She developed major engine problems on the way in, and underwent unexpected repairs whilst in dock. Her overhaul was complete and she was ready to exit drydock, until over-zealous actions from the tugs towing her out resulted in a crash into a sea wall. She damaged her stern and had to re-enter the dock for repairs. As the *Clansman* desperately needed to head to Aberdeen for her own refit, the *Hebridean Isles* became the relief vessel at Stornoway until the *Isle of Lewis* was repaired. CalMac suffered a logistical nightmare as vessels were shifted around the network to keep the routes running properly.

Only a return to using diesel oil would have helped the *Isle of Lewis*'s reliability, as the change to the heavier grade was thought to be severely damaging the state of her mechanics. On 6 March, she suffered a cooling pump failure whilst in heavy seas in the Minch. In July, following two further failures, Comhairle nan Eilean Siar were determined to work with CalMac to investigate why the *Isle of Lewis* was failing so often. CalMac also worked with the engine manufacturers to identify the issue, with possibilities including a design flaw in the twin Mirrlees Blackstones which had let her down so badly on so many occasions. However, CalMac insisted the change of fuel was not the cause, as the ship had been running on a lighter version known as Ulmer for the previous two months. In the meantime, her piston crowns were once again replaced before she managed to return to service, and thankfully suffered no further problems. The 2012 season ended on a high note for her, in stark contrast to what had gone before. She was even chosen by Ships Monthly magazine as the Ship of the Month for their December 2012 issue, which proved that even through breakdowns, she was able to garner some praise for her efforts.

Hebrides Takes Charge

The 2013 season began well for the *Isle of Lewis* and it seemed that she had finally left her run of breakdowns behind her. On 21 January, she took some time to berth at Stornoway on her 1315 arrival from Ullapool as strong winds reduced her manoeuvrability. Her remaining sailings that day were cancelled anyway due to the adverse weather. The *Isle of Lewis* was ready to leave Stornoway at the end of the month for her annual overhaul, at Leith in Edinburgh for the first time. January was in fact a month of firsts, as her relief vessel for 2013 came in the shape of the *Hebrides*, chosen in August 2012 as the main winter relief ship for the major routes in the network, a role usually assigned to her sister, the *Clansman*. The reason for this reshuffle was that the *Clansman* was to be kept at Oban, in order to reduce potential delays on the Outer Isles runs and keep capacity levels there in check. The Islay ferry, the *Finlaggan*, took the place of the *Hebrides* on the triangle from 1 December 2012. Just after 1400 on 25 January 2013, the *Hebrides* arrived in Stornoway for the first time to carry out her third relief stint during the winter period, having already relieved at Mull/Colonsay and Arran. After lying off outside the bay to allow the *Isle of Lewis* to depart for Ullapool, the *Hebrides* undertook successful berthing trials at No. 3 pier. She then remained tied up on the other side of the pier for the rest of the day, taking over from the *Isle of Lewis* at 0700 the following morning, allowing the regular vessel to head to Leith for overhaul.

From 26 January to 15 February, the *Hebrides* proved a huge success on the Stornoway-Ullapool route, giving a passage time of 2 hours 50 minutes, only five minutes slower than the *Isle of Lewis* considering her 16.5 knots compared to the regular's 18 knots. Controversy arose however, when on 29 January, the *Hebrides* had to abandon her evening sailing to Stornoway after ninety minutes of sailing, as the harbour there had closed due to horrendous Force 11 winds. She thus returned to Ullapool and remained tied up. She was then criticised on the grounds that her safety equipment was not suitable in winds higher than Force 6.

Meanwhile, the *Isle of Lewis* began her overhaul in Leith, having arrived there on the morning of 27 January. Whilst in drydock, she underwent a £700,000 refurbishment programme, where the main starboard engine was completely stripped down and re-built with brand new bearings. Her cooling pumps were changed to electric power, as the company who supplied the engine-powered versions were no longer able to do so. Following safety concerns about children being injured in the soft play area, this was converted into a puzzle and games room, and seating in the observation lounge was also upgraded. On 13 February, the *Isle of Lewis* completed her refit and ran compass trials in the basin at Leith, where she met the Queen's former royal yacht, the *Britannia*. She then left Leith that evening to return to Stornoway, which she reached at 1630 on 14 February, berthing on the left-hand side of No. 3 pier. With the *Hebrides* finishing her penultimate day of her relief roster at Stornoway, 15 February was the only day for a photographic opportunity of the two vessels together. The *Hebrides* then handed the service back to the *Isle of Lewis* at 0700 the next morning, and headed south to Oban to relieve the *Clansman*.

The Western Isles Major Units having Problems

Once back in service, the *Isle of Lewis* began to arrive in Stornoway nearly fifteen minutes ahead of schedule. This was unusual but her refit was thought to have given her an extra boost. However, this joyful improvement came to an end on 7 March, when she suffered a turbocharger failure during her last sailing of the day to Stornoway. She was out of service for six days, because of delays in getting the spare parts flown in from Germany in time. It seemed that there would be no relief vessel for the route, until the *Clansman*, which had just completed her overhaul at the Garvel, came straight to Stornoway to take over the route until the *Isle of Lewis* was repaired. Over a month later on 10 April, the *Isle of Lewis* suffered a second breakdown on her 1350 to Ullapool. Luckily she had managed to reach Ullapool, so the spare parts did not need to be taken further, and she was back in service on the morning of 12 April, having run sea trials in Loch Broom the night before. Compared to her turbocharger problems in March, this was a much faster repair job.

However, the *Isle of Lewis* was not alone in having problems. Both the *Clansman* and the *Hebrides*, considered to be the most reliable of the current major units, were experiencing difficulties too. The *Hebrides* suffered a turbocharger failure of her own on her way back from overhaul in Birkenhead, and then broke down on three separate occasions during April after returning to service at Uig. Anger at these problems caused some North Uist businesses to accuse CalMac of 'trying to sink' them and demands for compensation were made for 'damaging' their 'livelihood'. But the truth is that breakdowns can unfortunately happen at any time, especially when you least expect them. Thus, 2013 did not turn out to be a vintage year for the Western Isles ferries.

Reconstruction Works at Ullapool

On 15 May, the *Hebrides News* website reported that major works at Ullapool pier, required to accommodate a larger replacement vessel for the Stornoway route and awarded to Dingwall-based company Wallace Stone, would mean that over the 2013/2014 winter period the *Isle of Lewis* might have to divert to Uig, Skye. This would be problematic because her draught was so deep that in the event of a low tide she would not be able to use the pier at all – she was restricted at many of CalMac's ports mainly because of unsuitable depth. The depth at low tide in Uig is four metres, whereas the draught of the *Isle of Lewis* is almost twenty centimetres deeper. In addition, her stern ramp would not be of any use, as it is off-set to port to suit Ullapool. If the *Isle of Lewis* berthed stern-in at Uig, the pier would be on the starboard side of the ship. When she visited Uig for trials in July 1995, she berthed bow-in during high tide, and left her stern out at a tiny angle in order for the bow ramp to land properly, with a few inches on the starboard side to spare.

In June 2013, during a Clyde River Steamer Club interview to celebrate CalMac's 40th anniversary, Martin Dorchester, managing director of

CalMac Ferries Ltd, was questioned about the *Isle of Lewis*'s possible redeployment somewhere else around the CalMac network, despite the great difficulty in doing so. Mr Dorchester said, "The obvious route is Mull, but we'd have to shift the loading doors. It sounds like a big thing, but it's only a matter of cutting steel. The challenge would come if we then needed to redeploy her back to the Ullapool-Stornoway route. We're working through that now." To fit the two linkspans at Oban and Craignure, the *Isle of Lewis*'s stern ramp would instead have to be off-set to starboard, which would most certainly have ruined her chances of being brought back to Stornoway as a relief vessel for her eventual successor. Without major modifications, the *Isle of Lewis*'s ideal redeployment route could instead either have been the Uig triangle, provided that dredging work was undertaken at Uig; or to replace the *Caledonian Isles* at Ardrossan and Brodick, provided that she used a brand new purpose built terminal at Brodick announced by CMAL, which would also need to be dredged to accommodate her deep draught. However, there were also reports later in the year that she might be sold to seek further service in Sweden, if her services were no longer required by CalMac. Considering her enormous size and her 'route-specific' status, this would have been the most sensible thing to do. These reports remained unconfirmed for some time to come, and she would later prove too valuable to be sold out of the CalMac fleet, as she was quite popular with enthusiasts and tourists alike.

A New Freight Vessel

Even though the replacement Stornoway ferry was due to enter service in 2014, the *Mùirneag* was due for replacement herself in October 2013, by which time her British safety standards were due to expire, and some sort of plan would have to be in place from then until 2014. Various candidates for the replacement freight vessel included the *Arrow*, which attempted berthing trials at both Stornoway and Uig. Another candidate was the *Arrow*'s sister ship, the *Clipper Ranger*, which was eventually chosen in August 2013, and she gave her first sailing on 22 September, after successful trials at both Ullapool and Stornoway on 19 September. After several days of lay-up in Stornoway, the *Mùirneag* departed for a new life in Istanbul, Turkey at 1000 on 3 October. She would be renamed

Stolt Swazi. Now the Stornoway ferry duo consisted of the *Isle of Lewis* and the *Clipper Ranger*, and it would remain this way until the autumn of 2014.

On 4 October, the *Isle of Lewis* was having a fine final few weeks of the 2013 CalMac summer timetable until she suffered a major mechanical fault that required her to visit drydock. Shortly after berthing at Stornoway on her last sailing of the day, divers had discovered a break in the starboard propeller shaft seal tube. This was similar to the problem she had suffered in the port shaft at Lochmaddy in April 1998, and could not have happened at a worse time, as the October school holidays were about to commence. The *Isle of Lewis* had to sail on one engine, just as she had done from Lochmaddy, from Stornoway to the Garvel drydock for repairs as the fault could not be corrected whilst she was still afloat. The *Hebrides* was chosen as her temporary replacement at Stornoway, having carried out extra sailings on her own station, the Uig triangle, with the *Finlaggan* taking up the triangle service again. The *Hebrides* arrived at Stornoway at 1215 on 6 October and immediately took up the 1430 Sunday sailing to Ullapool, remaining on the route until the following Friday.

After almost a week in the Garvel drydock for repairs to her seal tube, the *Isle of Lewis* was ready to return to Stornoway on 10 October, meeting various ships on her travels, such as two newly delivered ships for Western Ferries, and the new hybrid ferry for Raasay, the *Hallaig*, also built by Ferguson's of Port Glasgow. The *Isle of Lewis* re-entered service on 11 October on the 1350 to Ullapool. She had arrived at 0920, loaded traffic and passengers, and quickly moved to the other side of No. 3 pier to allow the *Hebrides* to unload, before departing, having picked up passengers and crew wishing to change over. The *Hebrides* then loaded her crew cars and set off for Tarbert to get back on the Uig triangle, so that the *Finlaggan* could get back to Islay. Everything returned to normal once again.

Ten

Bouncing Back

T HE *ISLE OF LEWIS* began 2014 going back and forth as usual across the Minch. Three weeks later, on 25 January, she was ready to depart for her overhaul once again. Returning to relieve her was the *Clansman* and they changed over at Ullapool prior to the 1815 sailing to Stornoway, which the *Clansman* undertook, leaving the *Isle of Lewis* to sail direct for Birkenhead, where she arrived in the early hours of Monday 27 January. Whilst the *Isle of Lewis* was in her element in drydock, the situation surrounding her fleetmates was to prove quite bizarre.

The *Clansman* had no major issues, other than berthing difficulties in the very strong winds of 27 January, however the *Clipper Ranger*, arriving as normal in Stornoway on the morning of 28 January, suffered a fuel problem, resulting in a severe blackout and causing her to lose all power. This soon resulted in very heavy contact with No. 1 pier. Her stern was badly damaged, and she was required to visit Birkenhead for steel plating repairs. The *Hebridean Isles* took over the freight service in her absence. The *Isle of Lewis* was delayed in leaving Birkenhead owing to turbo problems, but arrived in Stornoway at 2315 on 20 February, immediately re-entering service with the next day's first sailing at 0700. After completing her sailings on 20 February, the *Clansman* left Stornoway two hours before the *Isle of Lewis* returned, and sailed directly for Gourock to undertake her own overhaul at Garvel.

When the *Isle of Lewis* re-entered service, she had further bad luck. One of her rudders seized during her first sailing back in service and she was forced to sit at Ullapool awaiting repairs. The *Isle of Arran* was summoned from her refit at Garvel to take over. The troublesome rudder was removed before she returned to Birkenhead, the only facilities available to her. She arrived back in Stornoway at 1440 on Thursday 6 March, re-entering service yet again the following morning. There had been complaints from locals and Comhairle nan Eilean Siar that the *Isle of Arran* was too old, slow and small to be a relief ship for Stornoway, despite being a reliable 'workhorse', and that CalMac should consider using a larger ship – the *Clansman* or *Hebrides* – to cover any breakdown eventuality. The *Isle of Arran* carried out another brief stint at Stornoway on 1 April, providing the first return trip that morning when the *Isle of Lewis* suffered a less severe issue in her electronic control gear on 30 March. The fault was fixed by 1 April, allowing her to return to service a delayed 1350 sailing to Ullapool that afternoon.

On 21 April, the *Isle of Lewis* was involved in a rescue mission off Cailieach Head near Scoraig during her 1025 run to Stornoway. It was reported that two canoeists had been blown away from shore as their canoe came round the Head. The *Isle of Lewis* temporarily halted her passage, and diverted to Cailieach Head to assist a search, also involving a coastguard helicopter and the Lochinver lifeboat. After some time the canoeists were found on the opposite side of Gruinard Bay at Mellon Udrigle, safe and well following their ordeal. The *Isle of Lewis*, the helicopter and lifeboat were assisted by two other vessels. After the canoeists were picked up, the *Isle of Lewis* continued on her regular passage to Stornoway, despite being delayed by about 35 minutes as a result of the rescue mission.

No. 3 Pier Closed

From the afternoon of 8 May 2014 onwards, the *Isle of Lewis* started using No. 1 pier at Stornoway, a result of the closure of No. 3 pier, which was being heavily redeveloped to suit the requirements of the new ferry on order to replace her. The redevelopments included a brand new Passenger Access System (PAS), the installation of new Yokohama fendering and a complete overhaul of the marshalling and car parking areas. Similar works were carried out at Ullapool, with a 35 metre extension to the pier being installed there as well as a new PAS and fendering. The old berth at Stornoway was specifically modified for the *Isle of Lewis*. As only one

Stornoway linkspan was available now, a new changeover procedure was introduced. After unloading her traffic and passengers every night but Saturday, the *Isle of Lewis* moved to the Esplanade berth, thus enabling the *Clipper Ranger*, which had been anchored off out of the way for most of the day in order to give way to the regular ferry, to load her freight at the linkspan before leaving for Ullapool. Then the *Isle of Lewis* would return to the linkspan to load traffic for her first sailing every morning. This would remain the case until the redevelopments at No. 3 pier were fully completed.

From June to September, the *Isle of Lewis* met a selection of visiting cruise ships in what was Stornoway Harbour's busiest summer with visiting vessels for many years. One example was the 1972-built *Discovery* – built in Germany and operated by the Essex-based Cruise and Maritime Voyages Company – which made her visits to Stornoway on 10 June and 3 July. Another was the Fred Olsen-operated *Black Watch*, which made her visits on 20 June and 26 August. Several vessels were so enormous that they were unable to berth at the regular pier, so had to lie at anchor off Arnish or Sandwick Bay, and use their lifeboats to transfer the passengers to the pier at Stornoway. Some, however, were the correct size to berth at the pier without problems.

Eleven

Enter *Loch Seaforth* (II)

ON 8 JUNE 2012, a £42 million replacement for the Stornoway ferry was announced by Transport Minister Keith Brown MSP. The 116 metre long vessel was designed to carry 143 cars or twenty HGVs and 700 passengers, and to be more fuel-efficient, consuming 30% less fuel than the combined consumption of the *Isle of Lewis* and *Mùirneag*. She was also designed to be faster, with a top speed of 19.2 knots which would bring the passage time down by fifteen minutes, and more importantly, more reliable in adverse weather. It was rumoured that she would feature two sets of engines, so that if one set broke down, the other could be used as a back-up while repairs were being carried out, and the vessel could still sail at full speed. As a result, breakdown of individual engines would not affect the reliability of the ship. This could be achieved by using a combination of diesel-mechanic and diesel-electric engines, one set of each type. Such a set up would be a huge advantage over the *Isle of Lewis* and her consorts, all of which were not legally allowed to sail without two fully operating engines.

On 22 June, the order was placed with German shipbuilders Flensburger Schiffbau-Gesellschaft (FSG), a renowned leader in modern ro-ro shipbuilding, making the new ship the first CalMac vessel to be built in Germany. Caledonian Maritime Assets Limited, the state-owned company which owns all the CalMac ferries and charters them out to the operators – although the new vessel would in fact come under the ownership of the Lloyds Banking Group who would then lease her out to CMAL – stated that FSG had the most to offer; such as meeting efficient deadlines, displaying an ability to carefully study every aspect in full detail and also having a reputation for delivering each ship 'on time, within budget'.

On 21 January 2013, it was announced that the new vessel's main engines and auxiliary generating units were to be supplied by Wartsila, which had supplied the *Finlaggan*'s engines in 2011. On 20 August, however, it was revealed that she would feature a five-engine arrangement – two main engines and three auxiliary units. It had also been announced that the *Isle of Lewis* was to be retained as a back-up for the 'foreseeable future', until locals were entirely satisfied with the new vessel's performance, with her fate being decided as soon as her services were no longer required at Stornoway.

On 8 April, it was announced that the new ship would be named *Loch Seaforth*, the winner in a competition run by CMAL from 5 March until 5 April, from a shortlist of five names. The winning name received 40% of votes, beating *Callanish*, *Cape Wrath*, *Loch Broom* and *Loch Ewe*. The *Loch Seaforth* became the second MacBrayne vessel in over 160 years to receive the name, reviving that of the popular mail-boat which served Stornoway from December 1947 until January 1972. Ironically, *Loch Seaforth* had been one of many suggestions for the name of the *Isle of Lewis*!

Construction of the *Loch Seaforth* began on 16 September 2013, with the cutting of the first steel, and a ceremony was held to commemorate the event. A similar event was held to commemorate the keel-laying on 3 February 2014. Other sections of the ship, including the superstructure and bridge, were being built at Gdansk in Poland, and these were towed to Germany to be joined with the rest of the hull shortly after the launch. FSG had announced in late November 2013 that the *Loch Seaforth*'s delivery would be delayed by about two weeks after the roof of their building shed had suffered damage in a storm. Controversy arose too, when CalMac decided that the *Loch Seaforth*'s larger car capacity might mean the cessation of the third return trip in high summer, which had usually been provided by the *Isle of Lewis* on certain days of the week to cope with demand. In other words, this meant she would continue the exact timetable provided by the *Isle of Lewis*, while including the freight return provided by the *Clipper Ranger* in her roster too.

The *Loch Seaforth* was finally launched at 1120 on 21 March 2014. In a very fitting gesture from CMAL, she was christened by Mrs Joan Murray, the eldest daughter of Captain John Smith, who popularly served as master of the original *Loch Seaforth*. The new ship had been launched without her superstructure – which was on its way from Gdansk – and was joined onto the hull on the morning of 25 March. Fitting out then began immediately.

A Series of Delays

The *Loch Seaforth*'s introduction into the fleet, however, would sadly run into controversy. Drydocked at Odense in Denmark between 23 and 31 August for the painting of her underwater hull and work on her propeller hubs, her handover was delayed until October 2014, four months later than initially scheduled. These delays were partly the result of electrical problems during fitting out, but were mainly due to the horrendously slow progress of the major redevelopments at No. 3 pier in Stornoway; Ullapool being the first of the two terminals to be completed. Meanwhile, the new vessel undertook her sea trials out on the Baltic Sea between 25 and 29 September, where her unique five engine set-up gave her a very impressive top speed of 23.2 knots. The *Isle of Lewis* had all her records overtaken by her successor after nineteen years, with the exception of her beam; the *Isle of Lewis* was recorded as being 18.52 metres wide, with the *Loch Seaforth* twelve centimetres narrower. She was eventually handed over to CMAL on 10 October, despite FSG suffering financial troubles, which could have resulted in the vessel's ownership being determined through German courts. Fortunately, FSG found new owners in Siem Industries, and would therefore continue to build ships. The *Loch Seaforth* finally left Flensburg on 4 November, arriving on the Clyde three days later; she was to be laid up there until her new facilities were ready to receive her. Ironically, two thirds into her voyage, she passed off the Point Peninsula in strong southerly gales, which kept the *Isle of Lewis* stormbound in Stornoway for the whole day, whilst her successor proceeded at nearly 20 knots to Greenock. In fairness though, this sort of gale would have pushed the *Isle of Lewis* up north if she attempted to sail across to Ullapool. The *Loch Seaforth* made her first calls at Ullapool and Stornoway on 12 November and 6 December 2014 respectively. She carried out berthing trials with her stern ramp at the mainland port with success, and carried out crew familiarisation trials at Stornoway – performing several manoeuvres from Arnish to Goat Island – as the pier facilities were still not ready.

There was further controversy when plans for a complete replacement of the Ullapool linkspan with a two lane system were announced. This would involve the vehicle ferry service to Ullapool being suspended for six weeks, from 23 February to 7 April 2015. A temporary timetable for that duration would see the *Isle of Lewis* sail with vehicles and their drivers from Stornoway to Uig, with all timings being dependent on the tide. The *Clipper Ranger* remained on charter to carry out sailings for freight – also to and from Skye. This meant that the *Loch Seaforth* would not be able to commence a full service on the route until after the Ullapool pier was reopened. Chief complaints were that officials had not consulted anyone earlier than they should have. It was finally decided, however, that the problems in completing the works at Stornoway's No. 3 pier would now delay the start of the installation of Ullapool's new linkspan until 20 April. In reality this now offered the benefit of longer working hours during the replacement operation, which later led to the works being reduced down to four weeks instead of five.

A taskforce was set up to attempt to get the project back on track, with new Transport Minister Derek Mackay MSP stating that the *Loch Seaforth* would be fully operational at Stornoway by the end of May. SNP MP Angus MacNeil repeatedly called for the Ullapool works to be suspended until after the tourist season, in order to avoid losses for local business during the summer period when large numbers of tourists normally visit the islands. He was adamant that the works taking place in April and May would impact on this significantly. Stornoway Port Authority stated that the alterations to No. 3 pier would be finished in time for early February, with a view to bringing the *Loch Seaforth* into service by the middle of that month following successful berthing trials.

The *Isle of Lewis* meanwhile continued to provide a highly satisfactory service to her namesake isle as she entered her 20th anniversary year. She was relieved on 26 January by the *Isle of Arran*, whilst she underwent her overhaul on the Mersey. The *Isle of Arran* was chosen due to the fact she and the *Hebridean Isles* were the only other CalMac vessels, in addition to the *Isle of Lewis*, *Loch Seaforth* and *Clipper Ranger*, which were able to be use Ullapool's current linkspan as the new Yokohama fenders pushed the vessels further away from the pier than usual. The *Clansman* and the *Hebrides* – the larger relief ships which were regarded more favourably on the Lewis service than the smaller and slower *Isle of Arran* – would need to wait until the new linkspan was installed.

Home at Last

The *Loch Seaforth* appeared in Stornoway again on 2 February – permanently this time – and, after several months' delay, finally underwent successful trials at No. 3 pier two days later; testing first bow, then stern ramp. She spent her first ten days at her home port undergoing further trials. Tests a few days later confirmed that the new Passenger Access System fitted well too. The new vessel was in the company of the *Isle of Arran*, as the *Isle of Lewis* was taking longer than scheduled on the Mersey undergoing her overhaul. The *Loch Seaforth* gave her first fare-earning passage of the Minch during the early hours of 11 February by taking the freight run in place of the *Clipper Ranger*, to assess her overnight sailing capabilities. An open day for the public to explore the new vessel took place on 12 February, by way of two separate periods lasting two hours each; one in the afternoon and the other in the evening. She then gave her very first passenger sailings of the Minch the next morning, before handing back to the *Isle of Arran* for the afternoon sailings. The *Isle of Arran* would be ready to depart pending the return of a refreshed *Isle of Lewis* from Liverpool.

The *Isle of Lewis* was delayed in leaving the Mersey owing to propeller hub repairs, and so the *Loch Seaforth* was finally able to enter service on Monday 16 February – effectively covering for her predecessor – therefore giving her first full day of sailings on her published timetable, with the *Clipper Ranger* continuing on the freight roster, whilst the *Isle of Arran* remained on stand-by until the *Isle of Lewis* was able to return in case of teething issues. The *Isle of Lewis* finally returned to Stornoway on 1 March, sailing over to Ullapool later on that day to change crews. The following afternoon, she called at Uig for the third time in her lifetime, to carry out trials to ensure she would fit when the Ullapool linkspan disruption began. She berthed at the Skye port from 1440 to 1535, berthing bow-in first, then stern-in, but not testing the latter ramp. She was then laid up at Stornoway, standing in case of teething issues with her successor until the latter was fully settled in, and the two vessels would occasionally share the roster between them.

TWELVE

A New Future Ahead

THE *ISLE OF LEWIS* marked her 20th anniversary in 2015. Following her return from her overhaul at Birkenhead on 1 March, she lay up at Stornoway as a reserve to the *Loch Seaforth*, in case of any potential teething troubles. Her new status as a 'back-up' ship was immediately put to the test on 5 March when the new vessel suffered a ventilation fan problem on her way into Ullapool, and the *Isle of Lewis* had hurriedly to relieve her and perform an extra sailing overnight to get stranded passengers back to Stornoway. From the week of 16 to 20 March, she would carry out the days' sailings to allow the *Loch Seaforth* to undergo minor maintenance at Arnish yard. The final 'piece of the jigsaw' would be in place with the completion of the new Ullapool linkspan in late-May.

On 3 April, the *Isle of Lewis*'s life was interrupted when she was called to carry out an extra sailing on the Uig triangle to assist the *Finlaggan*, relieving for the *Hebrides*. The *Isle of Lewis* left Stornoway at 1230 bound for Uig, arriving and berthing bow-in four hours later. This extra voyage departed Skye at 1700 and the *Isle of Lewis* sailed to Lochmaddy for the first time since 31 May 1998, berthing stern-in at 1850 and discharging almost seventy vehicles. She had carried out her first ever passenger sailing to a destination other than Stornoway or Ullapool, and had done so with enormous success. I had the pleasure of being a special guest on the bridge and of witnessing this great event with pride and admiration, knowing – as a result of dredging work – that the vessel had proved not as route-specific has she had been made out to be. She left Lochmaddy for Stornoway again at 1915 for more lay-up. From 20 April to 18 May, she commenced the temporary vehicle service from Stornoway to Uig with only few weather disruptions, whilst the *Loch Seaforth* carried out passenger only sailings between Stornoway and Ullapool, with the *Clipper Ranger* taking freight to and from Uig. When the new linkspan at Ullapool finally opened, the *Loch Seaforth* was able to commence full service as promised.

As June began, the *Isle of Lewis*'s future with CalMac was still up for consideration, and so, in order to assess her long-term solution, she undertook a tour of the network to see which ports she would suit her best, and what alterations would need to be made to ensure she could berth at others. She would make her first ever visit to most of the ports she planned to call at. From 4 to 9 June, she visited Lochmaddy, Castlebay, Oban, Craignure, Brodick, Ardrossan, Troon, Campbeltown and Tarbert, Harris, with each visit varying in success, though giving great indications as to what could be done to suit other terminals. For example, her current configuration can only allow her to berth bow-in at Uig, berthing to port when bow-in, and the same principle applied to places like Tiree, Craignure and Ardrossan. At most other ports which allowed her to berth to starboard when bow-in or to port when stern-in, her current configuration would be left unchanged. Otherwise, her stern ramp could be moved to the starboard side for use at the 'right-hand side' piers. With the new, wider linkspans at Stornoway and Ullapool, any changes made to her ramp set up would not really dampen her chances of providing work on her old route, while she would be given the capability of providing extra sailings or relief stints elsewhere. The plan – later to prove false – was to carry out stern ramp amendments, and for the *Isle of Lewis* to take over the Oban-Craignure service from 2016 onwards.

For the time being, the *Isle of Lewis* was called on to provide extra sailings between Tarbert and Lochmaddy on 19 and 20 June after the Sound of Harris ferry broke down for two days in a row, and proved to be popular and useful on the triangle. On 23 June, it was announced a 24-hour strike would take place on 26 June as members of the RMT union were concerned about pay and work conditions arising from the political decision to choose who would operate the next Clyde & Hebrides Ferries contract; the contenders being CalMac and a subsidiary of Serco. In response, the *Isle of Lewis* moved to Oban to provide extra sailings to and from Castlebay on 24, 25 and 27 June. On 26 June, every major CalMac ship stopped working for 24 hours as expected, on a day that followed two days of 'work to rule' action. The *Isle of Lewis* provided an early 0046 sailing to Castlebay on 27 June, the same day as the popular Barrathon, and was praised for 'saving' the event from being cancelled altogether as a result of the strike action. She also called at Uig to carry out an extra sailing to Lochmaddy to allow vital goods to reach North Uist, whilst the *Loch Seaforth* carried out extra Stornoway sailings to keep the extra weekend return going which her predecessor would otherwise have provided. An unusual army charter from Uig to Lochmaddy followed on 12 July – this was the *Isle of Lewis*'s first military charter in over seventeen years.

Owing to these emergency sailings to Barra and calls at Skye and North Uist on the way home, the *Isle of Lewis* began her extra summer sailings between Stornoway and Ullapool a week later than originally planned, on 3 July. These sailings were carried out every Friday and Saturday until 29 August, providing extra capacity to supplement the *Loch Seaforth*, leaving Stornoway at 1030, and departing from Ullapool at 1430, taking an hour and fifteen minutes on turnaround on the mainland. She proved very useful in this duty, and seemed to running very close to capacity. She was also on hand to relieve the *Loch Seaforth* in case of any breakdown eventuality, such as that of 16 July, when the *Loch Seaforth* caught a creel in one of her propellers. Despite this she managed to carry out the morning freight run and the 0700/1025 passenger return by herself, and the *Isle of Lewis* took over from then until 2000, after which the *Loch Seaforth* returned to service with the freight return on the 17th. On Sunday 19 July, the *Isle of Lewis* undertook an extra 0700/1030 sailing to Ullapool and back to transport tourists home to the mainland following the 20th Hebridean Celtic Festival, whilst the *Loch Seaforth* spent time carrying out regular safety drills before undertaking the usual 1430/1830 return in the afternoon. This practice was repeated on Sunday 16 August, the day after the 8th Hebrides Car Rally; another annual event raising funds for Macmillan Cancer Support.

On the week of the 20th anniversary of her inauguration – 27 to 31 July – the *Isle of Lewis* was unusually not based at her home port for a few days. On 28 July, the *Hebrides* had the misfortune to suffer a rare breakdown during her 0940 sailing to Lochmaddy; an issue with one of her propulsion units. It was concluded that this would take two days to repair, and that the *Hebrides* would head to No. 1 pier at Stornoway for repairs, which would therefore allow the *Isle of Lewis* to take over the triangle, putting her July 1995 berthing trials at Uig, Lochmaddy and Tarbert to the ultimate test. She first undertook a special return sailing from Uig to Tarbert at 1345/1630, and back to Harris again at 1830, before sailing at 2015 to her overnight berth at Lochmaddy, which, of the three ports, had the most suitable tidal depth. The next morning, 29 July, the *Isle of Lewis* undertook a 0535/0730 return from Lochmaddy to Uig. Owing to the lack of tide at Uig until the early afternoon, the *Isle of Lewis* stayed at Lochmaddy, spending some time cruising off the North Uist coast until she berthed again to load for a 1330 sailing to Uig once the tide was high enough. She then sailed to Tarbert and back at 1530/1815, before returning to berth overnight at Lochmaddy once again – she was becoming very acquainted with North Uist! Meanwhile, the *Hebrides* underwent repairs at Stornoway, a port she had not visited since October 2013. She had berthed bow-in at No. 1 pier after 2100 on 28 July, whilst the *Loch Seaforth* loaded her freight traffic at No. 3 pier; the two vessels meeting for the first time. They met three times on 29 July, as the *Hebrides* did not leave Stornoway until 0600 on 30 July when her repairs were completed and she took over at Uig again after 0900. The *Isle of Lewis* undertook a 0715 sailing from Lochmaddy to Uig before handing the triangle back to her 'shipyard sister'. She left at 1700 to return to Stornoway, after remaining on the triangle for a while to make sure the *Hebrides* was fully back to normal.

On 17 August, the *Isle of Lewis* returned to Oban to carry out another series of sailings to Barra following the reshuffling of vessels to cover the breakdown of the *Finlaggan*. The *Clansman* focussed on extra sailings to Coll and Tiree, whilst the *Lord of the Isles* took over from the *Finlaggan* at Islay until she was repaired. The *Isle of Lewis*'s presence on the Barra service had its benefits; she was able to reduce the passage time between Oban and Castlebay by roughly twenty minutes and took four hours and forty minutes on each run thanks to her eighteen knot top speed. She also had much superior vehicle capacity – 123 versus the *Clansman*'s ninety – and she was able to give a dedicated service to Barra. She was unable to berth at Lochboisdale owing to the tight channel and small facilities at the South Uist port. This in turn put pressure on both the *Hebrides* at

Lochmaddy and the *Loch Alainn* at Eriskay, where most of the dangerous goods that the *Isle of Lewis* was unable to carry were transported in order to reach Barra. With order restored at Islay, the *Isle of Lewis* returned to Stornoway and on 29 August, gave her last supplementary return sailing to Ullapool and back at 1030/1430 – a route she had faithfully served since 31 July 1995. She was to return to that service again in late October when the *Loch Seaforth* undertook her first overhaul. On 30 August, the *Isle of Lewis* headed back to Oban to carry out more sailings to Barra, as it was now the *LOTI*'s turn to 'conk out'. Her arrival and departure from Oban that afternoon was captured by several photographers from the 'steamer's fraternity'. On 6 September, she took over the *Loch Seaforth*'s regular 1430/1830 Sunday return to Ullapool whilst the new ship carried out trials at No. 1 pier at Stornoway; first stern, then bow-in. At the same time Stornoway Port Authority announced major upgrades to No. 1 pier in order to fully accommodate the new ship, no matter which way she berthed, as she was fully unsuitable to use Tarbert as an alternative.

On 22 September the *Isle of Lewis*'s future within the CalMac fleet was confirmed. Transport Scotland announced new dedicated services as improvements to the network. First of all, Castlebay was to be served by means of a new dedicated return service from Oban, and the *Isle of Lewis* would be in charge of this. Another dedicated, albeit controversial, service to be introduced was a seasonal Mallaig to Lochboisdale service, to be undertaken by the *Lord of the Isles*. The *Clansman* would focus on serving Coll, Tiree and Colonsay from Oban, the *Coruisk* would partner on the Craignure service and likewise the *Lochinvar* would work the Mallaig-Armadale service alongside the *LOTI*. To deal with the problem of carrying dangerous goods directly to Barra – according to her passenger certificates the *Isle of Lewis* was unable to carry certain dangerous goods if she had 132 passengers or more on board – a logical solution was to retain the *Clansman*'s weekly excursion to Barra via Coll and Tiree, which proved popular with tourists. This would in turn free up space on the *Isle of Lewis* to carry more traffic from Oban and Castlebay. Modifications for the *Isle of Lewis*, carried out during her 2016 overhaul at Greenock, would include changing her bow ramp to be off-set to port to suit Oban's newer linkspan, the only one of the two she would fit at. It should also be noted that the ports of Coll, Tiree and Colonsay were tidally constrained for the *Isle of Lewis*, meaning she would have difficulty in berthing in case of providing extra sailings there. It also remained to be seen whether the *Loch Seaforth* would be able to cope with the Stornoway service on her own, as it had been repeatedly claimed she would not manage without the assistance of a second ship.

The *Isle of Lewis* would remain inactive and laid up at Stornoway until 28 October, when it was time for the *Loch Seaforth* to depart for her first ever overhaul, to take place at Birkenhead. In drydock, she was to be fitted with a new fuel management system which would apparently be more economical, and many of the other fleet members, including the *Isle of Lewis* herself, would be fitted with a similar system during their own overhauls. To get around the dangerous goods problem with the *Isle of Lewis*, CalMac announced that they had chartered the NorthLink freighter *Hildasay* to take over the freight roster. CMAL had been offered the chance to purchase the *Clipper Ranger* before her departure from the fleet in late-May, however this never came to fruition. The *Hildasay* arrived at Ullapool and Stornoway for berthing trials on 28 October, and undertook the freight service later that night. The temporary charter of the *Hildasay* was announced as a reciprocal arrangement between NorthLink and CalMac, as the *Isle of Lewis* was expected in turn to cover the Scrabster to Stromness route whilst the *Hamnavoe* had her own overhaul during the early part of 2016 – this took place from 29 February to 16 March 2016, with the *Isle of Lewis* providing a 100% success rate at her first attempt. Following the *Loch Seaforth*'s return from Birkenhead, she remained on standby at Stornoway, and provided assistance elsewhere when required as 2015 drew to a close. Although her full-time service on the Stornoway service had finished, she took her place as the new Oban to Castlebay ferry on 25 March, sailing successfully in spite of an amber alert with strong winds and swell on that first day. With that, the mighty *Isle of Lewis*'s presence within the Caledonian MacBrayne network is set to continue for many years to come.

Epilogue

THE *ISLE OF LEWIS*, introduced on the Stornoway to Ullapool service in July 1995, was one of the most significant vessels ever to serve the island port. She was not only the largest ship ever used on the crossing, but, until the construction of her successor, two decades later, was the giant of Caledonian MacBrayne. She was indeed a true Scottish vessel, to this day remaining the largest ever product of Ferguson Shipbuilders of Port Glasgow on the Clyde. Her top speed of 18.92 knots, which also made her CalMac's fastest motor vessel, made many regard her as a 'super ferry' during her early years of service. Although she may not have been as characterful, or remembered as fondly as, for example, the 1974 *Pioneer*, she certainly sealed her reputation during her nineteen years at Stornoway. She was popular, but latterly controversial, dogged as she was by repeated mechanical issues. She had the resilience, however, to bounce back, and resume her duties very swiftly indeed.

As a modern, roll-on/roll off car ferry, the *Isle of Lewis* was surprisingly attractive in her design and arrangements, with spacious, well-appointed, attractive lounges and ample open-deck space for her passengers. Ordered by CalMac during the reign of the late Colin Paterson, an enterprising and far-seeing individual, she brought into the fleet the latest styles in luxury and passenger comfort, as well as the latest measures in marine safety, with lessons learned from the *Estonia* and *Herald of Free Enterprise* disasters. The word most often used to describe her internal accommodation was simply 'spacious', with many thinking her as the *QE2* of CalMac. Her width of 18.5m, as opposed to the more usual 15.8m of other vessels and other factors including high fuel consumption on a long passage requiring unusually high speed, as well as a stern-ramp set asymmetrically off the midline meant that the 'route-specific' ship only ever gave a full passenger service between Stornoway and Ullapool. However, successful trials and special sailings on the Uig triangle and Barra routes suggest she might well have been up to the challenges of operating elsewhere.

In a community with a long tradition of 'moaning' about their boat, the *Isle of Lewis* was a regular victim of criticism of her capabilities, being the butt of jokes; the ship islanders 'loved to hate'. Despite this she provided the best possible lifeline service she could between the largest and most northerly of the Outer Hebridean islands and mainland Scotland. She had many admirers from those within the enthusiasts' fraternity; Ian McCrorie, Professor Donald Meek, Lawrence Macduff, the late Jim Aikman Smith, Colin J. Smith and many others. Considered a state-of-the-art vessel in 1995, she had begun to look a little 'tired' twenty years on. Her replacement, the vast *Loch Seaforth*, has now started a new exciting era in the history of the Lewis sea route.

In my opinion, the *Isle of Lewis* was a superb asset to the island which she served extremely well, and for which she was named. I salute such a fine ship for nineteen years of honest toil on one of Scotland's most important island ferry services.

Appendices

APPENDIX I: MEET THE CAPTAINS

The longest serving and perhaps the skipper most associated with the *Isle of Lewis*, Alex Morrison is one of Caledonian MacBrayne's most experienced sailors with a career spanning over forty years; as well as being the spitting image of Captain Bird's Eye, or Edward John Smith of the *Titanic*, thanks to his traditional captain's beard. Born on Lewis in 1950, Alex lives in Melbost Borve, on the north-west of the island.

He began his professional seagoing career in 1967 with Denholm Ship Management in Glasgow and was employed on various vessels including oil tankers, chemical and iron ore carriers, product tankers and general cargo ships.

He joined Caledonian MacBrayne in 1974, with his first duty for the company taking place on 21 March of that year, as second mate on the *Iona* – later the *Pentalina-B* – on the Oban-Craignure crossing to Mull, for what was initially supposed to be a temporary job. Since then, he has worked on almost every other vessel in the fleet at one time or another, such as the 1964 *Hebrides* – the first MacBrayne's car ferry – on the Uig triangle between Skye, North Uist and Harris.

He attained his Master's ticket in 1977 and in 1980 won his first command, of the new Small Isles passenger vessel *Lochmor*, built at Troon in 1979. Confronted with a Force Nine south-westerly gale, he cancelled his first scheduled sailing. A master of any commercial passenger vessel, let alone a CalMac ferry, is considered the company's representative onboard the vessel and is responsible in law for her navigation, the maintenance of an accurate log and the safety of all on board.

Prior to joining the *Isle of Lewis*, Alex spent time as captain of the *Hebridean Isles* on the Uig, Lochmaddy and Tarbert triangular route.

His appointment to the *Isle of Lewis* in April 1997 came in rather sad circumstances, as one of the original masters, Murdo Kennedy, a Kyle of Lochalsh native, was incapacitated by illness. Captain Kennedy later passed on, sadly, in February 1999. The four months that Alex was supposed to cover the *Isle of Lewis* became a decade as permanent master, from 1997 to 2007. Between 2007 and 2014, Alex alternated between the *Isle of Lewis* at Stornoway, and the *Hebrides* on the Uig triangle. Following two knee replacement operations, he returned full-time to the *Isle of Lewis* in March 2014, having now been associated with the good ship for over seventeen years.

Alex has many fond memories of his time on the *Isle of Lewis* – and some not so fond. In 1999, during an afternoon sail to Ullapool in a severe NNE gale, the *Isle of Lewis* was struck by two huge waves twelve miles out from Stornoway. Although not reacting in any violent manner, she began to surf on the waves, rolling from side to side in excess of twenty-five degrees several times. With this severe motion, Alex became concerned that something serious would happen. Sure enough, the Chief Engineer at the time, Brian Fraser, arrived on the bridge with a look on his face that made it apparent things were not at all well. "The shop is wrecked", Brian said. "Is it bad, Brian?" Alex replied. Brian responded, "Well, let's put it this way, Alex; if I were you, I wouldn't go down there to buy a paper just now!" It was found that the shop was an enormous mess, with sweets, souvenirs and so on strewn all over the floor, as a large display unit had fallen over. Initially it was feared that a child had been injured, but thankfully, this did not turn out to be the case. The display unit had not been bolted to the deck, but it would be firmly secured thereafter.

Another bizarre moment came in April 1998, during the first of the *Isle of Lewis*'s two Army charters to Lochmaddy during that year. One of Alex's colleagues and good friend, Donnie Finlayson, skippered the first sailing to Ullapool to collect the traffic. Alex then took over for the unusual passage from Ullapool to Lochmaddy, arriving early on Sunday 19 April. He had initially been expected to take the *Isle of Lewis* from Lochmaddy back to Stornoway to return home but the port propeller-shaft seized whilst manoeuvring away from the North Uist pier. The breakdown was serious, and the *Isle of Lewis* had to sail to Greenock for emergency repairs that took nearly a month. As Alex had no other clothes to change into, he was forced to go to the town centre at Greenock and buy some. He went home to Lewis a week later.

That November, too, Alex was in command when the *Isle of Lewis* called at Stromness on her way home from overhaul on the Tyne. CalMac was one of the bidders to take over Northern Isles services – then out to tender – and were eager to show off the pride of their fleet to the people of Orkney. Nearly 700 locals came aboard to admire her, and left impressed both by her and with the hospitality of Alex and the crew.

Alex has covered most major CalMac crossings over the last forty years, from Arran to Lewis. His commands have included the 1964 *Hebrides*, the *Columba* (converted into the *Hebridean Princess*), the *Caledonia*, the *Glen Sannox*, the *Arran*, *Bute* and *Cowal* – the ABC trio of ferries built in the 1950s – the *Pioneer*, the *Lochmor*, the 1951 mailboat *Loch Carron* and the *Isle of Arran*. He also served on the former Stornoway ferry *Suilven*, and had great confidence in her capabilities, not least her legendary seaworthiness. Despite her slow speed and sparse accommodation compared to the *Isle of Lewis*, she was indeed a great servant to the island, despite a large increase in commercial traffic in her final years on the route.

Alex believes that the current CalMac organisation – a fusion, for legal and taxation reasons, of Caledonian Maritime Assets Ltd, CalMac Ferries Ltd and David MacBrayne Ltd – if complex, gives an as good or better service than the old order, attested to by all the awards received in recent times. A slight concern, however, is that today's vessels are being overworked in what used to be the 'fallow' winter months with much more relaxed timetables. Four decades ago, for instance, there was only one return sailing daily between Stornoway and Ullapool off-season, sufficient for all traffic offering while allowing 'valuable maintenance downtime'.

Finally, Alex is sure that the future generation of CalMac captains is fully guaranteed, with all the experience of older company captains being passed down the line through men of his generation to younger officers. He also believes that there are many excellent young masters within the company at present – and I would be very inclined to agree with him.

APPENDIX II: TECHNICAL DETAILS AND ACCOMMODATION

The *Isle of Lewis* was the largest and fastest motor vessel ever constructed for Caledonian MacBrayne when she was introduced to the fleet in 1995, and remained so until the arrival in 2014 of the *Loch Seaforth*, her successor on the Stornoway route. Built by Ferguson Shipbuilders of Port Glasgow, she also became the yard's largest product to date. Known as yard number 608 during her construction, she took just under fifteen months to build, with the keel-laying taking place on 23 February 1994, and her launch by HRH Princess Alexandra following on 18 April 1995.

Although she was quite attractive for a modern car ferry, she was thought of by some as looking rather blunt and slab-sided compared with older style vessels. She was also noted for her tendency to sit awkwardly on the water, with one side lower down than the other. She also had an undoubted tendency to 'slam' at the bow when hit by strong waves in adverse weather, though this turned out to be a natural occurrence for her, and did not make her in any way unsafe or unseaworthy. As a result, she was usually a victim of criticism, with some believing her to be inferior to her predecessor, the *Suilven*. Despite these claims, the *Isle of Lewis* was always a safe and capable vessel.

External Appearance

In regard to her external appearance, the *Isle of Lewis* was a further development of the *Isle of Mull* and *Caledonian Isles*. She was also regarded as a much enhanced version of the *Lord of the Isles*, another Ferguson-built vessel. Like her two consorts, the *Isle of Lewis* had a fully enclosed car deck. She carried on her bow visor the trademark CalMac lion rampant, which was also found on the centre of each of her twin funnels. The shape of the funnels was based on an equilateral triangle. They were fully painted in red, with two pointed tips at the rear, and raked backwards and up, with a black section on top of each. Curiously, the black tops of the funnels had a smaller circumference than the red parts, which was unusual for a CalMac major unit. There was a large grill on the front of each funnel, initially bare during her first two years, and smaller ones under the tips at the rear. Forward of each funnel was a main motorised lifeboat, and twenty inflatable life-rafts; ten on each side of the ship.

The *Isle of Lewis* did not feature an external promenade deck forward, unlike the *Caledonian Isles*, but the addition of six windows forward, and three extra-large ones on each side of the observation lounge on Deck 5, made up for this, resulting in passengers being able to enjoy very scenic views of the Minch whilst having the opportunity to unwind and relax at the same time. The window layout on the *Isle of Lewis* consisted of two rows on each side. There were also three windows on each side, showing where the lounge bar at the stern was. Her bridge had nineteen windows forward, each with their own car windscreen-style wipers, and three on each side. Aft of the bridge on each side were small fast rescue crafts. During her 1999 overhaul, she received new framework and a new larger RIB-style fast rescue craft on the port deck aft of the bridge, which in my opinion spoilt her appearance slightly. Above the bridge and crew accommodation was a small yellow mast, on which featured a pair of traditional radar scanners; a Racal Decca system as originally fitted, which was then replaced by a more efficient SperryMarine system, which became standard on many CalMac vessels. On Deck 6 – above the Deck 5 rear crew accommodation block – was the large main mast, where the vessel's horn was found, along with the standard CalMac pennant. As standard on every vessel in the fleet, a Scottish saltire flew at the bow, with a British ensign at the stern.

Internal Accommodation

The *Isle of Lewis* was extremely well-appointed in terms of her accommodation. If an observer were to stand aft of the bar, and look straight down either side of the ship towards the cafeteria at the bow, he would be forgiven for thinking he was on board one of the great ocean liners such as the *QE2*. Local journalist Fred Silver, former editor of the Stornoway Gazette, stated in hyperbolic, though tongue-in-cheek, terms that he 'wandered in a daze from lounge to lounge, lingered in the long, wide corridors, paced out the restaurant to see how many football pitches could fit in, and, whenever possible, gasped with amazement'. He went on to describe how 'guests waded through plush carpets, passed the TV lounge, the children's play area and the special dog corner – complete with tiled floor and drain. They suffered exhaustion and agoraphobia crossing the entrance lobby'.

The main entrance concourse on the *Isle of Lewis* – situated midship – was originally and fully carpeted in blue and panelled in pink, and was actually larger than the *Suilven*'s main lounge. Also found in the concourse was a gift shop, information desk, and two stairways to the open decks above, as well as the two stairways from the expansive car deck. The commodious cafeteria, which occupied the full width of the forward section of the ship on Deck 4, was originally carpeted in grey and panelled in primrose, with sixty-seven sets of turquoise tables and chairs (fifty-four rectangular tables, and thirteen circular ones). The curtains in the cafeteria were patterned in various colours. During her 2004 overhaul, the cafeteria was renovated and the primrose panelling replaced with a creamier shade, although the original tables and chairs were retained. In later years, many of the tables and seats were removed to make way for an enclosed lorry drivers' lounge and ambulance room to port, and disabled seating and a reclining area to starboard. There was also a stairway on each side of the cafeteria leading directly into the observation lounge above. The lounge bar at the stern was originally panelled in pink, with the tables being the same colour. There was also blue seating and red carpeting, the seating being arranged in seven curved bays. After the 2004 refit, the colour scheme of the lounge bar would remain largely the same, although the carpeting was renovated, and the blue seating replaced with purple. The two corridors leading from the concourse to the bar had light-blue panelling and a darker shade of blue carpeting. Other facilities on Deck 4 included the original soft play area (which later became an over-eighteens' games room), female toilets and one of two dog areas to port, and to starboard, male and disabled toilet facilities, the second dog area and an invalid lift for disabled access from the car deck. There were also two sets of luggage racks, one on each side of the vessel. There was another stairway leading directly to the open decks just opposite the starboard dog area. Curiously, the shop and bar were closed in 2015 and the stock was moved into the cafeteria. However, the stern lounge remained open for use.

On Deck 5, also known as the boat deck, the spacious observation lounge was to be found. This sat directly above the cafeteria at the bow, and featured ten seating bays, and full size windows offering scenic views of the Minch; six forward and three on either side. The observation lounge was originally panelled in light blue, the tables being the same colour. The curtains and seating bays were purple and the carpeting green. There were also fifty reclining seats and toilet facilities aft to port, and the TV lounge and Coffee Cabin, serving light refreshments, aft to starboard. The chestnut coloured seating in the TV lounge could accommodate a hundred, and the panelling and curtains were originally fawn-coloured. In 2004, a new children's area, known as the 'Cub Club', replaced the original soft play area on Deck 4. This new area allowed parents to relax whilst also being able to observe their children playing at the same time. The original colour scheme of the observation lounge would survive the 2004 refurbishment, but during a similar renovation in 2008 the panelling was changed to purple, and the carpeting and seating were renovated; with new partitions being installed in the latter.

Aft of these areas was a small passageway with doors at each end leading out to the large external decks. This passageway was noted for its gallery of framed photographs of previous Stornoway vessels, such as the *Shelia*, the *Lochness*, the original *Loch Seaforth*, the *Pentalina-B* (ex-*Iona*), the 1964 *Clansman* and the *Suilven*, and a large framed image of the *Isle of Lewis* herself in the centre, taken in 1995. These photographs came from the collection of well-known 'steamer' enthusiast Lawrence Macduff.

The large external deck, which ran down both sides of the ship towards the stern, was where the funnels and main mast were to be found. There were large amounts of traditional red plastic seating; ninety-six on Deck 6 where the mast was found, and sixty-six on the main deck below, giving a grand total of 162 seats. Four external metal stairways led up to Deck 6.

Some unusual features of the ship included a nursing mothers' room, a wooden plaque with the vessel's name in English and Gaelic (*Eilean Leodhais*) on it, special doors leading into the cafeteria and bar which featured the CalMac flag engraved on frosted glass, and small guiding lights set into the floor in certain areas which would help in the event of smoke. There were also several tools for emergency use in case of fire on the ship, such as alarm bells, fire hoses and fire alarm call points. There were three Emergency Assembly Stations on the *Isle of Lewis*, and large signs in each station denoted this. Station A was in the cafeteria, Station B in the lounge bar, and Station C in the observation lounge. Another addition to the vessel, rather curiously, was a ferry door on each side of the hull, between the 'n' in 'Caledonian' and the 'M' in 'MacBrayne'.

APPENDIX III: GENERAL STATISTICS
AND TECHNICAL DETAILS

At 101.25 metres (332.18 feet – and also ninety metres between perpendiculars) in overall length, 18.52 metres (60.76 feet) in breadth, and with a draught of 4.19 metres (13.75 feet) and a moulded depth of 12.20 metres (40.03 feet), the *Isle of Lewis* became the largest motor vessel ever constructed for CalMac or the company's predecessors. With her top speed of 18.92 knots – as measured on her sea trials on the Skelmorlie measured mile – she was also the fastest ever. Her gross tonnage was registered as 6753, her net tonnage being 2242 and her deadweight 660 tons. No CalMac vessel built after 1995 and before 2014 surpassed any of the *Isle of Lewis*'s specifications, and so she held the honour of being the company's largest and fastest vessel for nineteen years; the longest of any in the fleet, before the *Loch Seaforth* surpassed her.

The *Isle of Lewis*'s main machinery consisted of two Mirrlees Blackstone K6 Major diesel engines, each of which produced a maximum continuous rating of 3266 kilowatts at 600 rpm. Before then, the standard engine for new major units for CalMac had been the Mirrlees Blackstone 8MB275. Given the *Isle of Lewis*'s intended service speed of eighteen knots, the engineers at Ferguson Shipbuilders, keen to continue CalMac's reliance on Mirrlees Blackstone, realised that the 8MB275 was too small an engine to achieve this speed. They decided instead, despite initial doubts, to install the larger, more elderly, but reliable design of the K6 Major. This was not originally a general marine engine, being more commonly used in power stations, such as the one in Stornoway. The vessel's design was then worked around this choice of engine, which may have contributed to the 'slamming' and vibrating tendencies experienced in rough weather. In addition to her main engines, she also had two Ulstein 1500 AGSC gearboxes, two Ulstein four-blade propellers and two 8.5 ton bow thrusters – powered by a separate set of two 350 bhp Caterpillar diesel engines – which gave her a trademark 'drone' that could be heard when arriving in or leaving port.

Her electrical system consisted of four 32kW main alternators and one emergency alternator at 322kW, 415/240V, 3 phase 50Hz. Her tank capacities were 100 tons for gas oil, forty tons for fresh water and 900 tons for water ballast. Other equipment included hydraulically-powered bow and stern ramps, bow visor and retractable stabiliser fins. Due to her increased 18.5m width, the ramps had to be very uniquely positioned. To unload successfully at Ullapool, the stern ramp was off-set to port, and to use Stornoway's former linkspan, the forward section of the bow ramp was off-set to starboard, although the bulk of the ramp itself was fixed in the centre of the ship. An interesting example of the implications of her ramp design occurred when she visited Uig, Lochmaddy and Tarbert for trials in July 1995. At Uig, she was able to berth bow-in, but hung the stern off the pierhead slightly to allow the off-set bow ramp to sit on the linkspan successfully, despite Uig's pier being arranged oppositely to those of Lochmaddy and Tarbert. The long pier at Lochmaddy, as well as the linkspan being placed on the correct side of the pier, gave her the most comfortable fit, allowing her to successfully test both bow and stern ramps at North Uist. At Tarbert, she was again able to berth bow-in without problem. As a matter of interest, when the *Isle of Lewis* first visited the triangle, the piers and Uig and Tarbert were shorter than they are now as they were not extended until 2000/01, in time for the *Hebrides* to enter service on the route in March 2001.

Safety and Capacity Details

During the *Isle of Lewis*'s construction, tragedy struck in the shipping world when the cruise ferry *Estonia* sank in the Baltic Sea in September 1994, with great loss of life. Following this disaster, safety measures were tightened in the European Union, and regulations for Safety of Lives at Sea (SOLAS) were strengthened further. The *Isle of Lewis* was the first new vessel for CalMac to be built according to these measures. Her internal bow structure had to be redesigned to meet these requirements, which were also the result of another high-profile marine disaster; the fateful capsizing of Townsend Thoresen's *Herald of Free Enterprise* off Zeebrugge in March 1987. The *Isle of Lewis*'s safety equipment included the two main lifeboats, each able to carry 150 people. In addition, there were twenty inflatable life rafts able to carry fifty people each – a grand total of 1,000 – as well as sixteen lifebuoys and 1164 lifejackets. In addition to her safety equipment, she also incorporated the latest developments in marine technology, such as computerised radar screens and various other navigational controls – including a system on the bridge to open and close the bow visor, and CCTV cameras and screens which allowed the bridge crew to observe activity on the car deck – a significant measure brought in following the loss of the *Herald of Free Enterprise*.

The *Isle of Lewis* was built to accommodate passengers and vehicles to a capacity fifty percent higher than the *Suilven*. She was designed with a Class IIA passenger certificate to carry 968 passengers and thirty-two crew; double that of the *Suilven*. However, this was reduced to 680, which was then permanently recorded as her passenger capacity limit. She was capable of carrying ninety-three cars or fourteen commercial vehicles on her main car deck, which was split into two sections and separated by a central casing, off-set to starboard slightly, with the result that there were three lanes to port, and two lanes to starboard. She was also built with two hydraulically-operated hoistable mezzanine decks, occupying the middle third of her overall length. Safety features on the car deck included warning sirens and flashing lights for the ramps and mezzanine decks and large 'No Smoking' signs on the walls at either end, and also on each end of the central casing. The stairways from the car deck to the passenger accommodation had a level section halfway, so that those using the mezzanine decks could access the passenger accommodation. Capacity on the mezzanine decks was eighteen cars on the port deck (three lanes of six), and twelve on the starboard deck (two lanes of six), adding another thirty cars to the ninety-three she could carry on the main deck. In terms of lane metres determining vehicle capacity, supposing the *Isle of Lewis* had none of her mezzanine decks deployed, the capacity was 240 lane metres plus only four restricted spaces for cars only. If the two-lane port mezzanine deck was used, capacity was reduced to 180 lane metres plus forty-one restricted car only spaces. Use of the three-lane starboard mezzanine deck saw capacity at 200 lane metres with sixty-four restricted spaces for cars only. If both mezzanine decks were utilised, than capacity would be at its tightest – with 140 lane metres and sixty-four restricted spaces for cars only. Therefore, the final maximum number of vehicles that could be accommodated came to 123.

Bibliography

To assist with my research, I have made use of the following publications and other material. Principally, I have used the various Annual Reviews by the Clyde River Steamer Club, spanning the years 1993 to 2011 – 1993 to 2003 being produced by Ian McCrorie, 2004 to 2006 by Stuart Craig, and 2007 to 2011 by John Newth. I have also made use of the several newsletters produced by Jim Aikman Smith and Derek Crawford for the West Highland Steamer Club.

Major Publications

Ian McCrorie; *Royal Road to the Isles*, Caledonian MacBrayne, 2001

Donald E. Meek & Nick S. Robins; *The Kingdom of MacBrayne*, Birlinn, 2006

Colin Tucker; *Steamers to Stornoway*, Islands Book Trust, 2013

Ian McCrorie; *Caledonian MacBrayne – The Fleet*, Caledonian MacBrayne, 2006

Ian McCrorie; *Caledonian MacBrayne – The Fleet*, Caledonian MacBrayne, 2010

Newspapers

Stornoway Gazette

The Herald

The Scotsman

Websites

Ships of CalMac

Hebrides News

Herald Scotland

The Scottish Government